The Only Wiccan Spell Book You'll Ever Need

For Love, Happiness, and Prosperity

Marian Singer and Trish MacGregor

Adams Media
Avon, Massachusetts

Published by Adams Media,
an F+W Publications Company
57 Littlefield Street, Avon, MA 02322
www.adamsmedia.com

ISBN: 1-59337-096-2

Printed in Canada

J I H G F E D C B

Library of Congress Cataloging-in-Publication Data
Singer, Marian.
The only wiccan spell book you'll ever need / Marian Singer and Trish MacGregor.
p.   cm.
ISBN 1-59337-096-2
1. Witchcraft. 2. Magic. I. MacGregor, T. J. II. Title.
BF1566.S514 2004
133.4'4—dc22
2004004810

Portions adapted and abridged from *The Everything® Wicca and Witchcraft Book* by Marian
Singer, © 2002, F+W Publications, Inc.; and *The Everything® Spells and Charms Book* by
Trish MacGregor, © 2001, F+W Publications, Inc.

This book is available at quantity discounts for bulk purchases.
For information, please call 1-800-872-5627.

Visit our home page at *www.adamsmedia.com*

Contents

Introduction

GIVEN THAT THIS spell book is *The Only Wiccan Spell Book You'll Ever Need*, you might be surprised to find it's not a hefty, verbose tome, filled with ancient magickal utterings or lengthy digressions exploring every detail of Wiccan belief. Perhaps you were even anticipating a gigantic storehouse for ingredients, an endless string of spellcasting recipes, or a slew of magickal charms and incantations. Something that purports to be *The **Only** Wiccan Spell Book You'll Ever Need* offers an awfully grand promise, after all. And yet, this volume is rather slim.

That's because there is no easy way to explain Wicca in a nutshell. Wicca is an ancient practice, a gentle, earth-oriented religion that seeks truth and understanding, and a way of life meant to affect inner change. Yes, it's a framework for using magickal powers. It also involves worshipping ancient Pagan deities, and it recognizes the duality of the Divine as one force that incorporates male and female, both God and Goddess. It encourages respect for nature, stresses concern for the planet, and acknowledges that the life force should be reverenced in all things, as well.

Beyond exploring basic tenants such as these, however, there is no need to devote chapter upon chapter to engraining the teaching and belief system of Wiccan practice. Because there is no rigid dogma in Wicca, it's not incompatible with other spiritual practices. Whether you come to Wicca from a base of traditional religion or no formalized religion at all, you can easily work Wicca into your life. Following Wicca and casting spells are highly personal experiences. Just as there is no single method for practicing Wicca, there are also very few rules set in stone when it comes to spellcasting. This doesn't mean there are *no rules,* mind you. For one thing, spellcasting must always seek the good of all—both for yourself, and for others—and it cannot cause any harm. (You'll learn more about these basic, core principles in this book.)

The point is, however, that the spells included in this book are merely meant to be representatives that show you what spellcasting entails and how it is accomplished. The beauty of this book is that you can use its guidelines as a springboard for exploring your own ways of doing things, and eventually begin to craft your own spells as your facility for spellcraft progresses and your knowledge and experience increase.

Magick is always present in all of us when we are young. We simply lose sight of it as we grow into adults and get swallowed by the stresses of day-to-day living. This book is about learning to reconnect with that magick. In these pages, you'll learn to pay attention to nature—the cycles of the moon, the power of the elements. You'll also discover how to incorporate nature's tools—crystals, stones, herbs, flowers, minerals, and such, into your magickal workings.

As you're using this book, realize that Wiccan spellcasting is not about magickal power in the stereotypical sense. There's no "hocus pocus" or "abracadabra" involved here, no stirring bubbling cauldrons or flying on broomsticks. The true magick of Wicca lies in developing your own inner potential and spirituality. Remember that deep inside yourself, you already have the power to tap into the energy of the universe and the natural world around you; you just need to recognize that potential and direct it. This book is intended to help you on your journey toward getting in touch with nature, in touch with the Divine, and in touch with your inner potential, because, ultimately, that is where the real value of spellcasting lies.

Part 1

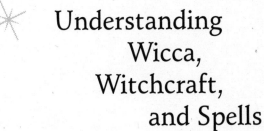

Understanding Wicca, Witchcraft, and Spells

Chapter 1

The Philosophy and Ideology of Wiccan Spellcrafting

BEFORE YOU CAN IMMERSE YOURSELF in the study of spell-crafting, it's important to sort out fact from fiction when it comes to Witches and Wiccans. First of all, Witches do not eat babies, and they're not Satanists who sell their souls to the devil in return for special powers. (This is a folkloric image that has been picked up by mainstream religions.) Most Witches and Wiccans are more ordinary than you might think—they drive cars rather than ride broomsticks and prefer pizza over eye of newt any day.

These sorts of stereotypical myths and misunderstandings need to be dispelled in order to understand the true ideals, ethics, and philosophy of Witchcraft. In reality, very few generalizations hold true when it comes to describing a Witch's powers or point of view. For instance, not all Witches have psychic abilities, as is often assumed. While some psychics might be Witches, not all Witches are psychic. And not all magick practitioners are modern worshipers of ancient Gods and Goddesses. This description is fairly accurate for Wiccans, but not always for Witches.

Only education and understanding can uproot misconceptions and prejudices about Witchcraft and Wicca, and in reading this book, you are on the right path. It's time to start thinking of Witches and Wiccans in a new sense—as people who are simply living their lives in a uniquely magickal way. We'll begin by examining the basic ground rules and core concepts that most Witches and Wiccans hold in common.

Witches and Magick

For the purposes of simplicity, the word *Witch* will be used to describe both male and female Witches or Wiccans throughout this book. Keep in mind that a male Witch or Wiccan is *not* called a Warlock. He is a Witch or Wiccan, too. *Warlock* came from an Old English word for *oath breaker*, and later, during the mid-1400s, came to mean *liar*. This is a rather nasty insult! The words *Wizard* and *Sorcerer* can also be used for a man or a woman. *Wizard* derives from a term meaning "wise," and *sorcerer* means "Witch" or "Diviner."

☀ Wiccan Wonderings: What, exactly, does Wicca mean?

Wicce, the Anglo Saxon word meaning "one who practices sorcery," is the root of the words Witch and Wicca. At first the term was applied to both wise men and women, especially those who practiced herbcraft (sometimes called "cunning arts"). After the Crusades, however, the term was used mostly for women and carried negative connotations. ◆

As a point of interest, the word *magician* is also appropriate for both sexes and for Witches as well as Wiccans. The ancient Persian prophet Zoroaster taught priests who were called *Magi,* and they relied heavily on astrology as an art. Depending on the cultural setting, *magician* came to describe people adept in astrology, sorcery, or other magickal arts. Note that the word *magick* in Wicca and Witchcraft is spelled with a *k,* to differentiate it from stage magic (or sleight of hand).

Which Is the Witch?

While folklore, literature, religion, and other cultural influences through the ages have often portrayed Witches in a negative light, history indicates otherwise in most cases. Despite the ugly face that these points of reference have tried to put on Witches, few, in reality, used their knowledge and abilities toward negative ends. Their heritage is that of helping and healing individuals and communities.

Most Witches learned their skills as a craft—part of a family tradition in which they were carefully trained. Villages and cities alike had honored, cunning folk to whom people would turn for all kinds of help—from encouraging crops to grow to mending a broken heart. In exchange for such services, Witches might receive a chicken, a measure of grain, or other necessities.

There was rarely any specific ethical or religious construct involved in Witchcraft unless it came from family or cultural influences, or from the individual's own sense of right and wrong. Witches do not need to believe in divine beings in order to use magick. They do not necessarily have a particular "code" or tradition to which they adhere, unless it is dictated by familial custom. This does not mean all Witches are without ethics or religion. Magick is simply a means to an end and is morally neutral (except in terms of how it's wielded).

Where Wicca Comes In

Writers like Gerald Gardner and Sir James Frazier are commonly given credit for coining the term *Wiccan* and kick-starting the modern movement in the 1950s. Although the methods and tools of the Wiccan are often the same as those of the Witch, the constructs within which Wiccans work are a little different. The primary variance is that Wicca is considered a religion, with specific rituals and moral codes similar to those of other world faiths.

Wiccan Gods and Goddesses

Many Wiccans follow a specific God or Goddess, and others honor several deities. These beings or personages may be chosen by the individual, or dictated by a group, magickal tradition, or a cultural standard. In this case, the Wiccan looks to the Divine as a copilot in the spiritual quest and as a helpmate in effectively and safely guiding magickal energy.

Several divine figures show up as popular favorites in the Wiccan community. Among them are:

Apollo (Greece and Rome)   Herne (Celtic Europe)
Brigid (Celtic Europe)   Ishtar (Middle East)
Dagda (Ireland)   Isis (Egypt)
Diana (Rome)   Pan (Greece)
Hecate (Greece)   Ra (Egypt)

Karmic Law

Another difference is that Wiccans and Witches view the cause and effect of their magick in different ways. Although Witches may or may not concern themselves with the potential results of a spell or ritual, Wiccans' intentions are bound by the Threefold Law, meaning that whatever they do, whether for good or harm, it will come back to them three times over. This doesn't mean Witches don't respect magickal power, nor does it mean Witches are unethical. It just means that Wiccans pay particularly close attention to the laws of Karma.

This saying, popular among Wiccan practitioners, probably expresses it best:

Bide the Wiccan law ye must
In perfect love, in perfect trust,
Eight words the Wiccan Rede fulfill:
An' ye harm none, do what ye will.
What ye send forth comes back to thee,
So ever mind the Rule of Three.
Follow this with mind and heart,
And merry ye meet, and merry ye part.

Personalized Magick and Ritualistic Witches

One commonality that Witches and Wiccans do share is that both approach magick in personal ways—ways that can be incredibly complex or very simple. Kitchen Wiccans and Hedge Witches, for example, rely heavily on pragmatic, uncomplicated magick, much of which originates in folklore and superstition. Hedge Witches traditionally do not belong to a coven (a group of thirteen Witches). Solitary practitioners, they depend on self-study, insight, creativity, and intuition as their main guideposts. Hedge Witches may be self-dedicated, but they are rarely publicly initiated. Similar to village shamans and cunning folk, they provide spells and potions for daily needs.

Some Witches practice magick with more ritualistic overtones, drawing inspiration from the Kabbalah (Jewish mysticism and magick) and other mystical and spiritual movements. Ritualistic Witches, for instance, approach every aspect of a spell as if it were part of a huge puzzle: Each piece needs to be in the right place for everything to work as it should. For example, the astrological phase of the moon should be suited to the task, and every part of the working should be carefully constructed to build energy toward a desired goal. Workings such as these have been used for a long time and are honored as part of the tradition from which the Witch originates. That is not to say that a ritualistic school has no room for variety or improvisation. It's just that the improvisation usually happens within a set framework.

Are You a Good Witch or a Bad Witch?

What's the answer to this classic question? Are there "bad" Witches who use their knowledge and power for personal gain and ill will? Yes, of course there are, just as there are "bad" Christians, "bad" Muslims, and so on. If you shake any figurative tree hard enough, a couple of rotten apples are bound to fall. That's just human nature. The good news is that these rotten apples are the exception, not the rule.

Just like everyone else, Witches confront issues that require them to make ethical choices. For instance, should magick be used as a weapon, even if it's only to fight back? Wiccans and Witches alike see magick as gathered from the life energy in all things. That energy is

The Wicca Creed

As the leading Neo-Pagan author Starhawk writes in *The Spiral Dance*, "Love for life in all its forms is the basic ethic of Witchcraft. Witches are bound to honor and respect all living things, and to serve the life force." This code includes:

1. Preserving the Environment.
2. Honoring yourself and others.
3. Seeing sexuality as "numinous and sacred," part of the life force.
4. Understanding "What you send, three times over."
5. Knowing that we have the right to control our bodies.
6. Honoring the Goddess. "The Goddess has infinite aspects and thousands of names—She is the reality behind many metaphors. She is reality, the manifest deity, omnipresent in all life, in each of us."

then turned and directed by the Witch toward a goal. It's how each person uses magick that makes it white (positive, constructive, helpful), black (negative, destructive, harmful), or gray (not completely black or white). Defining these things in concrete terms isn't easy, however, because each person's perception of what constitutes white, black, and gray isn't always the same.

The White Magick Codes

White Witches (those who abide by a simple code that instructs them to work for the good of all) follow certain general guidelines. For example, as previously mentioned, many believe in the Threefold Law, which basically translates to *what goes around comes around, not just once but three times!* This is good reason to make sure your motivations are positive.

White Witches believe it's highly unethical to attempt to manipulate another person's free will with magick. This kind of manipulation occurs most commonly in love magick, if one person tries to force another's attentions. The problems inherent in this practice are obvious—a Witch who casts a love spell will always wonder if the object of her affection truly loves her, or if it's just the magick! In any case, this type of spell is selfish; it is certainly not cast for the good of all.

You won't find any spells in this book that harm anyone or anything. Remember, the Threefold Rule holds true especially for spells that seek to harm another.

With a spell, you're attempting to stack the odds in your favor—or in another person's favor. You're attempting to influence something in the future. We do this constantly, of course, through the power of our beliefs, but when you cast a spell, you bring your full conscious and creative awareness to the process. So remember your mother's advice: Be kind to others and be kind to yourself.

To ensure ethical practice, many Witches use a universal motto in prayer, spellcraft, and ritual: "For the greatest good and it harm none." Magickal people recognize that while the human mind and spirit have unlimited potential, the ability to recognize all possible outcomes of their magick is *not* unlimited. Human beings are not omniscient, and sometimes good intentions lead to terrible results. The universal motto, therefore, acts as a request for higher (and wiser) powers to direct the magick toward the best possible outcome, so that energy is not inadvertently misdirected.

✦ Wiccan Wonderings: Where do Witches go when they die?

Christianity has heaven. Buddhism has Nirvana. Many Witches believe that their souls go to Summerland, a resting place before reincarnation into a new body, in an ongoing cycle of birth, life, death, and rebirth. Although the idea of reincarnation cannot be validated, many Witches seriously consider the karmic implications of their actions or inactions. Reincarnation and karma teach that the past affects the present, and the present affects the future—no matter what life cycle you are talking about! ✦

Finally, both Witches and Wiccans believe in religious tolerance and respect every path as having potential for human enlightenment. Since people are different, it only stands to reason that the paths they choose to walk are different. In keeping with this outlook, you will never find a Witch or Wiccan standing on a street corner preaching about magick or faith. Both groups believe that people must choose their own path. In fact, by virtue of coming from other religious backgrounds, many Witches and Wiccans have done exactly that.

This brief overview is a broad generalization at best. Each Witch relies heavily on his or her inner voice or conscience in decision-making and in the way he or she wields magick. Witches believe that each person creates his or her own destiny by action, inaction, karma, and so on. There is no cut-and-dry answer to whether anyone is a good or a bad Witch, but most Witches hope to be the best Witches they can be!

Living and Thinking Globally

The world view of most Witches bears striking similarity to those walking a Shamanic Path. Like shamans, they see the earth as a living, breathing classroom to honor and protect, not a place to conquer and control. Every living thing in this world has a spirit, a unique energy pattern, including the planet itself. As a result, Witches tend to think globally, mindful of nature and the cosmic universe.

Earth as a Classroom

The Witch's body houses his or her soul. Since most Witches believe in reincarnation, their time on this planet is spent gaining and applying spiritual principles to stop the cycle of reincarnation eventually and return to the source. Witches regard the earth, its creatures, and its elements as teachers that have the power to reflect the divine plan and pattern that extends throughout the universe.

With this in mind, most Witches strive to weave their magick and live their lives within natural laws, working in partnership with the planet instead of fighting it. Many Witches are strong proponents of protecting endangered lands and wildlife, feeling that these losses not only eliminate a wonderful learning opportunity but also are a crime against Gaia (one name for the earth's spirit; in Greek mythology, Goddess of the earth).

Many Witches will donate their money or time to ecological causes in the hopes of educating and inspiring others to do likewise. Stewardship of this planet doesn't end with donations or recycling efforts, though. It also extends into magickal practices. Witches often send out positive energy from spells and rituals. The energy may be aimed at protecting a particular environment or species, or directed like a healing balm at the whole world.

✳ Wiccan Wonderings: What happens if someone important in your life is opposed to your spellcrafting?
Arguing about it is the worst thing to do. You're not going to change anyone's opinions about spells or anything else. Your best bet is to follow your practice in private. If possible, step back from the situation and ask yourself what in you has attracted the opposition. Try to look at the other person as a teacher. What is the lesson to be learned from the opposition? ◆

"It's sacred ground we walk upon with every step we take," many Witches sing. We need to move gently, to respect all life, and to honor the sacredness in all things and in each other. Otherwise, we are not truly honoring our magick.

Above and beyond caring for the environment, how else does this kind of global thinking affect Witches? Mostly in the way they perceive things. A rock, a flower, an herb, a tree, a stray animal may all hold special meaning, depending on when and where it appears and what's going on in the life of that person. For example, if a wild rose suddenly grows in a Witch's yard, he or she might take it as a positive omen of love growing in the home. Taking this one step further, the clever Witch would thank nature for its gift, dry some of those petals, and turn this little treasure into love-inspiring incense! In this manner, a Witch will often discover that walking a magickal path reinspires a childlike wonder toward the planet and the small things that are often overlooked in our busy lives.

A Word about Spellcasting

In the next chapter, you will learn some basics about what is necessary for casting spells. Always keep in mind that the most important elements in a spell are your intent and passion, not the words or the ritual. Once you have a grasp of the basics, you can design spells for any situation.

Remember, when casting any spell, it's always wise to open with a prayer for protection of yourself and others. This prayer can be from a traditional religion or one that you create yourself. Make such a prayer your opening ritual.

The following Zen prayer is actually the first spell you're going to cast. This prayer, said for someone in need, is simple, powerful, and at least 2,500 years old. It's most effective when you say it without being attached to the outcome. By saying the prayer, you're acknowledging that a higher force is at work and that force or power knows what is best for the person for whom you're saying the prayer.

Think of this as a boost to the spiritual immune system—it increases a person's available energy. When you write it out, jot the name of the person for whom you're saying the prayer at the top.

May He Be . . .
May he be filled with loving kindness.
May he be well.
May he be peaceful and at ease.
May he be happy.

Chapter 2

Belief, Intent, and the Magickal World Around Us

Snow White, Cinderella, The Wizard of Oz, Alice in Wonderland, Beauty and the Beast, Peter Pan, Star Wars. For most of us, these stories are where we first discovered spells and potions, Wizards and Witches, and the never-ending struggle between good and evil. Fairy tales showed us a world filled with magick—one where inanimate objects like mirrors, stones, and gems can have special powers; animals can talk; plants can think; and with a sprinkling of dust, kids can fly.

Then we, like Peter in the movie *Hook,* grew up and forgot about magick. Our lives became a little less rich and our imaginations started to shrivel as we got mired in the mundane details of our daily lives. Every now and then, we recapture some of that early magic through books and movies like *ET, Lord of the Rings,* and *Harry Potter.* But usually, we have to be *reminded.*

Did Arthur *really* pull the sword from the stone? Did Peter Pan *really* fly? Is Harry Potter *really* a Wizard? Who knows? The point is that we recognize the magick in such stories. That recognition somehow transforms our perceptions, however briefly, of what might be possible if we, like Peter Pan, *believed*.

Belief is the core of any spell. Without it, all you have are words and gestures, light and dust, nothing but bluster—rather like the Wizard that Dorothy and her companions exposed to be just an ordinary man. But what, exactly, is meant by belief? Go back to Oz. The Lion sought courage because he *believed* he was cowardly. That belief ruled his life until the Wizard pointed out how courageous he actually was. The Lion, as silly as it might sound, experienced a radical shift in his *beliefs* about himself when he realized that he had possessed what he desired most all along. Believing he *didn't* have courage is what crippled him.

✳ **Wiccan Wonderings: Are complicated spells better than simple spells?**
One isn't better or worse than the other. The complexity or simplicity of a spell should fit the situation and the desired result. If your life is busy and you're already pressed for free time, then simple spells may suit your lifestyle better than complicated rituals. ✦

Most of us are just like the Cowardly Lion. Maybe, for instance, you want abundance. To you, that means financial abundance, money in the bank, freedom from worrying whether the next check you write is going to bounce. But to those around you, your life appears to be incredibly abundant—you have a loving family, wonderful friends, a job you love. Sometimes, a shift in our deepest beliefs happens because someone whose opinion we respect or someone whom we love points out that we really do have what we desire. Other times, we reach the same conclusion on our own. In either case, the end result is the same: Our beliefs shift, and ultimately, our reality changes.

The Power of Your Beliefs

A belief is an acceptance of something as true. In the 1400s, people *believed* the world was flat until Columbus proved otherwise. In the 1600s, men and women were burned at the stake because people in power *believed* they were Witches who consorted with the devil.

On a more personal level, each of us is surrounded by the consequences of our personal beliefs. Your experiences, the people around you, your personal and professional environments—every facet of your existence, in fact—is a faithful reflection of a *belief*.

Some common ingrained, limiting beliefs that people hold onto include:

- I'm not worthy (of love, wealth, a great job, whatever).
- I'm a victim.
- My relationships stink.
- I can't do anything right.
- Happiness is what other people experience.
- People are out to get me.
- My health is bad.
- Money is the root of all evil.
- I can't do it (start a business, sell a book, whatever).
- I'm trapped.
- I'll never find the significant other who is right for me.
- I live in an unsafe world.

There are as many limiting beliefs as our imaginations can conjure. The foundations for many of these notions are laid in childhood, when we adopt the beliefs of our parents, teachers, and other authority figures. Childhood conditioning about beliefs can be immensely powerful. Inside the man or woman who lacks the sense of self-worth lurks a small child who may believe she's a sinner, untrustworthy, or not good enough.

On a larger scale, our beliefs are also gleaned from the cultures and societies in which we live. A woman living in the West, for example, won't have the same core beliefs about being female as a woman in, say, a Muslim country.

A belief system usually evolves over time. It's something that we grow into, as our needs and goals evolve and change. Even when we find a system of beliefs that works for us, we hone and fine-tune it, working our way deeper and deeper into its essential truth. Everything we experience, every thought we have, every desire, need, action, and reaction—everything we perceive with our senses goes into our personal databank and helps to create the belief system that we hold in this instant. Nothing is lost or forgotten in our lives.

We don't have to remain victims of childhood conditioning. With will, intent, and passionate desire, we can define for ourselves what we believe or don't believe, what we desire and don't desire. We can define our own parameters.

Invisible Beliefs

Most of us have lots of "invisible beliefs." These are deeply rooted beliefs that are largely unconscious and often so powerful that despite our best intentions and conscious desires, we can't seem to make headway. The challenge is to bring these beliefs into conscious awareness and work to change them.

One of the best ways to identify these invisible beliefs is to take an honest look at the people and experiences in your personal life as though they were a mirror of the beliefs you hold. Does your boss continually overlook you when it comes to promotions? Do your coworkers ostracize you? If so, perhaps you have an invisible belief that you're not worthy. If you continually attract relationships riddled with problems and drama or you attract abusive relationships, then perhaps the deeper belief also has to do with your lack of self-worth.

If you don't like what's happening to you and would like to change certain elements in your life, then it's advantageous for you to reflect on what you believe in order to identify the beliefs that are holding you back and the beliefs that are beneficial to your goals. Figure out which beliefs are *really yours*, as opposed to beliefs you learned from someone else and unconsciously adopted as your own.

If you're not sure about your belief system, the time to define it is before you begin casting spells—not after you've started. Once you know what you believe, it's easier to define your parameters, your boundaries, and the lengths you will go to attain something. It also helps in determining what you won't do, and establishing your bottom line.

Start by taking inventory of your life and writing down as many of your beliefs or preconceptions about yourself as you can. Zero in on your negative assumptions, and turn them into positive affirmations instead. By writing down the positive affirmation, saying it to yourself over and over during the day, and backing the affirmation with emotion, your unconscious will eventually begin to believe it. Once your unconscious believes it, the process of change and transformation begins to show up in what you experience.

Describe Your Beliefs

In 200 words or fewer, describe your beliefs, your own personal code. If you're not sure about your belief system, simply list what you think you believe. ✦

It's not necessary to make radical changes in your life—although it always helps to make a physical gesture that affirms your new belief. Simply begin to question why you do certain things, and you'll start to uncover your invisible beliefs about yourself and about how life works.

Your Personal Code

Every magickal tradition, from the Druids to Wicca to Santería, has its own code—principles that guide the practitioner, boundaries that he or she won't cross, a core of beliefs that permeates everything he or she does. These core beliefs define the parameters of the magickal practice. In Wicca, the primary principle is to harm nothing and no one.

But individuals also develop their own personal codes. Have you defined yours? As previously noted, cultural differences have a hand in sculpting a particular individual's beliefs. In the end, however, each of us must refine our own code as we evolve from children raised in the belief systems of our parents to adults who decide for ourselves what we believe.

This is not to say that any of us is omnipotent, that any of us has all the answers or even a good chunk of them. We're all seekers and we all have a need for some sort of belief system.

Your belief system may include an adherence to an organized religion or to some other spiritual discipline, or it may not include any sort of spiritual ideas at all. But at the heart of any belief system lies a code by which you live your life, and it may not have any connection whatsoever to other people's concept of good and bad. After all, even thieves have codes.

Do you believe in an afterlife? In a supreme being? In good and evil? Do you believe that reality is exactly as it appears, that what you see is what you get? Do you believe people can't be trusted, that all Dobermans are vicious, that it's every man for himself, that you're a victim and there's nothing you can do about it? Then your experiences will confirm those beliefs.

If, on the other hand, you believe that nothing is fated, that your free will and your innermost beliefs effect your reality, then your experiences will confirm that, too.

Because you have picked up a book on magick and spells, you probably already believe that you can shape your own destiny and are looking for practical information on how to do it more efficiently and pragmatically.

Magick is one route. But there are hundreds of ways to get to where you want to be. The bottom line of any exploration is defining what you believe and what works for you.

A New Understanding of Magick and Spells

We tend to think of magick in two distinct varieties—stage magic, such as the type that magician David Copperfield performs; or ancient magic, the sort attributed to figures such as Merlin. But the magick we're talking about in this book is simply the type you can use to manifest what you desire.

In the movie *What Dreams May Come,* the character played by Robin Williams dies and then wakes up in the afterlife. The place looks, smells, tastes, and feels more or less like the so-called real world. But he quickly learns that in this place, whatever he thinks or desires is manifested instantly. *All of it is a construct of consciousness.*

In casting a spell, you use that same sort of magick. The manifestation may not be immediate—although it can be. If your belief and your intent are strong enough, if you bring passion to your spell, if you can focus your consciousness toward a specific goal, and, most importantly, if you don't seek to harm anyone or anything by casting the spell, then the chances are very good that you'll achieve what you want.

Intent and Desire

The purpose of a spell is to manifest something that you need or desire. That need or desire (or both) comprise your intent. When you cast a spell, your intent is as vital to your success as your beliefs. What are you trying to accomplish? What's your goal? What outcome are you seeking? How badly do you want what you're trying to achieve or accomplish?

Defining your intent isn't difficult. Most of us do it all the time. On any given day, we make dozens of choices that manifest in any number of ways, and we do it without the ritual of casting a spell. We don't always recognize it, but our intent constantly creates magick in our lives. Despite our astonishment and delight when magick happens in our lives, we usually write it off as a mere coincidence and eventually forget about it.

Defining What You Want

This should be easy, but for many of us it's not. When you get right down to it, most of us know what we want *right this instant,* but don't have a clue about the bigger picture. We're mired in the trees and can't see the forest. As you're thinking about what it is you really want to accomplish with your spells, be honest, and take your time. Remember, the universe is never in a rush.

As you read through and cast the spells in this book, refer back to the brainstorming you did earlier in this chapter. The first hint you'll get about whether your beliefs are changing will be apparent in the quality of your experiences and relationships. You might notice that people are reacting to you differently and your life is opening up in unexpected ways.

How the Natural World Fits In

If you are serious about using magick and spells, you need to get in touch with the natural world around you. Although our everyday experiences might make it feel as if our "natural world" is the world of computers, the Internet, and offices sealed against the elements, this isn't the case. It's the wind blowing through your hair as you take a walk by the light of a Full Moon. It's the birds that live by the lake nearby, the trees that your kids climb, the flowers and the herb garden that you plant during the summer. The natural world is just as natural as it ever was, except there's less of it than there was twenty-five years ago, and most of us don't make enough of a point to enjoy it.

Take the time to rediscover the natural rhythms around you and the way they affect the flow of your inner life. If you don't do this periodically, you'll burn out and start to feel out of sync with everything around you. You need time out to go within.

These natural cycles that we seek when we take time out are vital to success when casting spells. As the saying goes, "timing is everything"—and that timing is tied to the lunar calendar.

Spells and Lunar Cycles

Every month, the moon goes through eight distinct phases. For the first two weeks of a given month, from New Moon to Full Moon, the moon is waxing, or increasing in size. This is a good time for casting spells dealing with manifestation and expansion. From the Full Moon to the next New Moon, a period of about two weeks, the moon is waning, or shrinking in size. This time is optimal for spells dealing with decrease.

Who, you ask, would want to cast spells to decrease something, when most of us are seeking abundance? But if, for instance, you want to decrease your responsibilities at work or at home, casting a spell during the Waning Moon makes a lot of sense. Likewise, if you're looking to streamline your life, decrease your debt, tie up the loose ends in a relationship that no longer satisfies you, or lose weight, these spells should all be done under the Waning Moon.

The New Moon is the time to plant symbolic seeds that represent whatever you're trying to create in your life. This is the time to cast spells for launching a new business, diving into an artistic project, starting a new relationship, or trying to get pregnant.

In any given month when there are two New Moons, the second one is called the Black Moon. It is considerably more powerful than a regular New Moon, so any seeding spells you do under a Black Moon might manifest more quickly.

The Need for Gratitude

In spellcraft, as well as life in general, gratitude is one of the most valuable attributes you can develop. It's imperative to accept all the good things and the compliments that come your way with a gracious thank you. Realize that this is the universe acknowledging your special individuality. Gratitude is intrinsic to any spell, so always end your spells with an expression of thanks. ◆

The Full Moon is generally considered the time of harvest, when you see the fruits of the seeds you planted at the New Moon. It's the best time to concentrate on the culmination of those spells. If your intent and desire are strong enough, it's possible to see the results of your New Moon spells by the subsequent Full Moon, a period of about two weeks. Or, you might not see results until several Full Moons later. But you *will* see results. Spells for healing and empowerment are best performed during a Full Moon.

The Blue Moon, the name for the second Full Moon in a given month, is a particularly powerful time for focusing on spells you did at the New Moon.

The odd and wonderful thing about timing your spells according to the phases of the moon is that it makes you more aware of them. How many times have you gazed up at a slivered moon and wondered whether it was waxing or waning? Probably not very often. Once you begin casting spells, that will change. There may even be subtle differences in your body rhythms, fluctuations in your menstrual periods, your libido levels, your hormones, or the level of your intuition.

The moon, after all, is our closest celestial neighbor. It influences ocean tides and blood tides. It is intimately connected to the ancient worship of Goddesses, to the Druids' rituals, to the Wiccan practices. In astrology, the moon represents the feminine, energy that is yin, the mother, and nurturing, emotion, and intuition. It is our most direct link to the collective unconscious. Once you find your lunar rhythms, you're able to tap your link to the Divine.

Darkness

Darkness is the time to cast spells, but forget the images you have of the three Witches in *Macbeth*, stirring their cauldron and cackling under the light of a Cheshire cat moon. Darkness in the real world isn't like that at all. For many of us, the moment when the sun goes down marks the beginning of the time we spend with the people we love, doing the things we love. In the modern world, darkness usually means the end of the work day, the cessation of light, and winding down (or up, if it's Friday). Unless you work swing or graveyard shifts, darkness is the time that belongs to you.

In a deeper sense, though, darkness marks a perceptual change. Our imaginations spring to life; we hear and see things that the noise and light of the day obscures; our intuition is sharper, more vivid. All of this adds to the mystery and wonder of all that is *possible* instead of confining us merely to what we think we know. In darkness, your beliefs shift more easily and often shift in bold, dramatic ways.

This doesn't mean that spells cast during the daylight hours are spit in the wind. The universe, after all, doesn't care when you make your wish. It's just that in darkness, it's easier to imagine *what might be*, and the capacity to imagine is integral to the success of any spell.

Common Concerns

Before you get started with your own spellcraft, there are a few common concerns that should be clarified:

First off, yes, spells do often work, but there are certain instances when they don't. For one thing, you can't force another person to do something that isn't in alignment with his or her highest good. You can curse, hex, or cast spells on someone to fall in love with you until you're blue in the face. But if loving you doesn't align with that person's highest good, nothing is going to happen.

✳ **Wiccan Wonderings: How often should a particular spell be done?**
Always give your first spell a reasonable amount of time to work—several days to a month. If nothing is happening, revise the spell or your intent. If you're still having problems, just release your desire. Quite often, the act of releasing something brings what you want. ✦

If a spell doesn't work, it might also be that your intent isn't strong and clear enough, or you haven't put 100 percent of your emotions behind it. Not to mention that we sometimes wish for things that aren't in our best interest. A spell is never going to work if what you want isn't in *your* highest good.

But who or what determines what is in your—or anyone's—highest good? That answer goes by different names: the higher self, the soul, the grander self, All That Is, the Goddess, God . . . . Whatever you call it, the central idea is that when you look in the mirror, the reflected image is a fraction of the whole picture. Somewhere in each of us is something, some type of energy, that grasps the whole picture.

Much of the time, we lose sight of things as our lives get bogged down in the details. According to esoteric thought, however, each of us has a blueprint of our lives, a kind of master plan, that we designed before we were born. We set up certain events and encounters to provide the types of experiences that would help us evolve. Whether we keep these appointments with destiny is up to us, and that's where free will comes in.

If you've applied the above criteria and your spell still isn't working, then perhaps you're asking for too many things. You should determine what's most important to you, then ask for just that. Sometimes, just rearranging the wording of a spell fixes the problem.

Another possibility is that you haven't given the spell enough time to work. How much time is enough? This is a sticky point. A spell that is in alignment with your highest good, backed by intent, clarity, and passion, can work immediately. For a complex spell that involves several people, the spell may take longer. Give it at least a month if it's complicated and a couple of weeks otherwise. Or, break the complex spell down into its components and simplify it.

Also be sure to re-evaluate your goal if it changes. If your goal has remained the same, then perhaps you should try the spell again, but with renewed passion and greater clarity about what you want. The more passion and emotion you put behind a spell, the greater the chances that it will work quickly.

Remember not to invest too much energy in the outcome of a spell. Once you cast your spell, forget about it. Release it, then let the process unfold. Trust that you'll get what you want. Casting spells is meant to be done in a spirit of fun and adventure. If your spells don't seem to be working, take a closer look at your mood. Are you approaching it too seriously? If so, then lighten up.

Chapter 3

Creating Sacred Space

BUDDHA ONCE SAID, "Wherever you live is your temple if you treat it like one." Most Witches and Wiccans would agree. Sacredness is more a matter of attitude and behavior than it is of trappings, and it certainly requires no building or props. Nonetheless, creating a sacred space to practice magick is important, and there are tools and processes Wiccans use to create magickally safe havens for their efforts.

In Wicca and Witchcraft, spells are often performed in a Circle, and group work, especially gatherings in which there are public rituals, frequently takes place in a circular "sacred space." A Circle shows that each person present is important to the success of the overall working. The Circle also represents unity, accord, wholeness, and a safe psychic sphere within which all can find comfort and protection.

Power Spots

Before you cast a Circle, you need to find your own power spot, because where you do your magick is as personal as the kind of magick you do. Some people prefer a specific spot that remains intact from the casting of one spell to the casting of the next. Others have no such loyalties and move their spot around—the yard one night, the garage the next. Find the spot that feels most comfortable and gives you some privacy if you live with other people or have pets. Cats are especially curious about anything new going on where they live. They may be Witches' familiars, but chances are they'll try to get into your incense and candles, too!

Interior Places

Some people favor power spots with a minimum of furniture and *things*, others like being surrounded with objects that remind them of magick and enchantment. It's up to you. If you're going to be casting a Circle for your spells, find a spot that's large enough to do so. Create an atmosphere that is calm and peaceful, and remove anything that might disturb that atmosphere. It helps to cast spells in an area with a pastel floor and walls. If the floor in your space is tiled or wood, find a throw rug or pillow that complements or matches the colors of the walls. You can also use it to sit on during your magickal work.

✦ Wiccan Wonderings: What is a Book of Shadows?

Also known as a Grimoire, this is a handy reference item. A Witch's guide and magickal diary, a Book of Shadows is what Witches use to record their observations and experiences. It includes everything from successful spellcraft formulas to the proper preparation of potions and timing for talismans. The Book of Shadows is akin to a bible for the Witch, who will turn to it again and again for insights, ideas, and tried-and-true recipes. ✦

In addition to a throw rug, pillow, or something else to sit on, you'll need a surface of some kind on which to work and put things. It can be as casual as a wooden box or a board propped up by bricks, or as ornate as an altar (you'll learn how to build your own altar in sections to follow). It's all a matter of personal preference. If the surface is used for other purposes, smudge it before you use it—burn sage and allow the smoke to suffuse the area.

If you have a favorite object—a statue, a stone, a crystal, or anything else—keep it in the area where you cast your spells. Consider it the guardian at the gates, a power object that will maintain the magickal atmosphere even when you're not there. You might want to use a small object, so you can move it easily. That way, your magickal atmosphere will travel with you. Even if you don't have a spot that's perfect, don't lose any sleep over it. Simply bring your intent, passion, and belief to any spell you cast, and you'll be on the right track.

Outside Locations

Finding a power spot in nature requires some time and intuition. Even if you decide to cast spells no farther than your backyard, you still need to find a spot that feels right. You can do this by walking the yard or the area you've chosen elsewhere and being alert to any unusual or intense body sensations: heat, cold, a chill, a cozy warmth in the pit of your stomach. Listen to those sensations, and you'll know which spot is right for you.

Dowsing is another way to find the right spot. Dowsing was originally used to locate water. The idea is that a forked stick or some other tool is used to sense the location of whatever you're looking for, so it dips down to pinpoint the best location. Use the forked branch of a willow, if you can find one, or make a dowsing rod from wire hangers. For any dowsing tool to work, though, it should be infused with your intent and purpose. Request aloud that the dowsing rod locate the right spot for your spellcasting.

Creating the Proper Ambiance

The casting of a protected, sacred space keeps out unwanted spiritual influences, purges the air of negative vibrations, and instills a sense of positive purity. The sphere of energy around this space also holds any magick created within it firmly in place until the practitioners are ready to release and guide the magick outward. The time spent creating sacred space is an important psychological ally for the participants, allowing them to adjust their thoughts and attune them to matters of Spirit rather than flesh. That attitude is important to the success of even the simplest magickal process.

Only a focused Witch can harness the energy to enact the intended effects, so creating a successful sacred space means having the right overall surroundings for whatever is going to take place. The following guidelines will help you create the right ambiance for your sacred space:

1. Ensure you (or the group) won't be interrupted.
2. Choose the right space for your task, taking into account weather, personal time, or physical constraints, and what's going to take place in the sacred space once it's created.
3. Make sure the area is safe and tidy; get rid of anything that will distract you from the task at hand.
4. Set up your tools so they're readily accessible.
5. If you light candles, make sure they are not a fire hazard. Keep them away from flammable materials (like curtains).

Casting Your Circle

Since ancient times, circles have symbolized both power and protection. When you cast a Circle, you're working on several levels simultaneously. On a physical level you're defining the boundaries for your work, and on a spiritual level you're imbuing the space with your personal power. In *The Spiral Dance,* Starhawk describes the Circle as "the creation of a sacred space . . . Power, the subtle force that shapes reality, is raised through chanting or dancing and may be directed through a symbol or visualization. With the raising of the cone of power comes ecstasy, which may then lead to a trance state in which visions are seen and insights gained."

The Circle, then, is intended to contain the power you conjure. As in any magickal work, you bring your beliefs with you into the Circle. If you believe in demons or evil forces, then your Circle also serves as a protective device, a wall between you and whatever you perceive to be evil. Try to get rid of that belief, if you can, before you cast any spell.

Your Circle should be large enough to accommodate the number of people who will be working inside of it, any objects that will be in the Circle, and your work surface. It should be cast clockwise (or deosil), so that when it's completed you'll be inside of it. Make sure you have a compass with you—you'll use it to determine the four cardinal points, covered later.

✳ **Wiccan Wonderings: Must a Circle be cast each time a spell is done?**
In some magickal traditions, the casting of the Circle is such an integral part of a spell that not doing so is the equivalent of, well, heresy! Nevertheless, do what feels comfortable. Some people enjoy the ritual of casting a Circle or have a belief that urges them to do so. But if this ritual doesn't appeal to you, or your beliefs tell you it's appropriate to do a spell without casting a Circle, then that's fine. ◆

The Circle may or may not be visible in any magickal working. It all depends on the practitioner and the overall goal of the working. Sometimes the wards are set directionally by words and actions alone. Other times there are functional altars set up at the four quarters to honor the powers there. (The four quarters are the four main compass points of the working space; you'll learn more on this in sections to follow.)

In ritual magick, the Circle may actually be drawn on the floor. Some people use flour to cast the Circle, others use sea salt. In the absence of either of these, dirt, chalk, stones, brick, or a moat of water will serve the same purpose.

The substance you use to draw the Circle is less important than the inner feelings and concentration you bring to the act. Remember: Everything in spellcasting is symbolic. When defining the boundary of a sacred space, the item used to create the physical perimeter should match the theme or goal of the magick to be worked. A Witch working a love-oriented spell, for instance, might release rose petals between each altar point.

Building an Altar

Generally, there is at least one central altar in a sacred space. Some Witches believe it's important to place their altars in the east (although there seems to be no explanation for this preference). For practical purposes, placing the main altar in the middle of your Circle makes more sense. Participants can gather around it, and a central candle can symbolize Spirit as the guiding force and nucleus of all assembled.

✦ **Wiccan Wonderings: Is an altar necessary for doing spell work?**
Not necessarily—it's a matter of personal preference. If the presence of an altar troubles the people you live with or gets in the way, you can either put the altar in your own personal area or somewhere outside, if weather permits. If it seems too difficult to set up an altar space, simply don't have one. ✦

The items and symbols you bring to the altar largely depend on the function of your magick. For example, for a ritual to honor your ancestors, you might want to include their photographs or personal effects. No matter the goal, it's a good idea to cleanse all the things you plan to use beforehand. One option is passing objects through the smoke of purifying incense such as cedar or sandalwood. Work regularly with your tools, both inside and outside of your sacred space, so they resonate with your personal energy imprint.

A Circle Within a Circle

To honor the elemental powers and the four corners of creation, some magick Circles have four mini-altars, one at each quarter. Wiccans frequently place items that represent the elements of each quarter in the corresponding corners of the sacred space, to honor those particular energies. As you cast the Circle and reach each of the four cardinal points, place the object that represents the appropriate direction. Once your Circle is closed (finished), face the east and focus

The Elements

The four elements are intrinsic to casting a Circle and to magick in general. They have magickal properties, just like anything else you'll use in spellcasting, and they act as conduits of your will.

The following chart provides a simplified guideline to those properties:

Elements and Their Correspondences

Element	Direction	Color	Object	Quality
Air	East	White	Incense	Expression, communication
Fire	South	Red	Burner	Passion, initiative, energy
Water	West	Blue	Cup	Emotion, intuition
Earth	North	Black, green	Bowl	Grounding, stability, security

When you cast your Circle, you can mark the cardinal points with any of the items listed in the "object" column or with a candle of the appropriate color. You can also use any other objects that are personally meaningful, which represent that element. Improvise, and have fun with it.

In the east corner, you might place a piece of aventurine or tin, a yellow candle, a feather, or frankincense and myrrh. Following clockwise around the outside of the Circle to the south corner is the fire altar, which might house a piece of amber, a red candle, marigolds, or woodruff incense. In the west corner, suitable altar decorations might include a seashell, a blue or green candle, coral, vanilla incense, and a bundle of chamomile flowers. And in the north corner, you might use a potted plant, a green or brown candle, a piece of moss agate, and some patchouli incense.

on the object that <u>represents that direction and that element</u>. Then turn south, west, and finally north and do the same thing.

There are several ways you can prepare yourself for invoking the quarters and all the magick to follow:

- Make sure you're well rested and mentally and physically healthy. Negative feelings undermine the success of any magickal effort.

- Take a ritual bath or shower before entering the Circle. This symbolizes washing away unwanted thoughts, tension, and energies. If this isn't possible, rinsing your hands in rose water (for perfect love) is a good alternative. Leave a bowl and towel near the entryway to your magickal area for this purpose.

- Dab your pulse points and third eye (located in the middle of your forehead) or the candles you plan to use with an oil that represents the purpose of your ritual or spell. For example, if you're raising energy to improve a divinatory effort, choose jasmine or marigold—both enhance psychic abilities. This anointing acts as a magickal aromatherapy. (See more on incense, oils, and candles in Chapter 4.)

- Breathe deeply in through your nose and out through your mouth at least three times, evenly and slowly. Relax and release, making sure your mind and spirit are focused and centered, and your motivations are sound. This way, you won't be handling magickal tools and symbols with any lingering "bad" vibrations in your aura.

- Say a prayer. If you're working with a group, ask everyone to breathe together and join hands to unite wills and spirits before praying. The prayer doesn't need to be fancy, just sincere, to welcome Spirit as a helpmate to the magick you're about to create.

Calling the Quarters

Calling the quarters creates an invisible line of force that marks the space between two worlds—the mundane and the spiritual, the temporal and the magickal. This boundary usually begins in the east (where the sun rises) and ends in the west, creating a complete Circle around, above, and below the practitioner. The only time calling the quarters begins elsewhere is during banishing (when it often starts in the north and progresses counterclockwise to decrease negative energy), or when another quarter is more important or significant to the working.

For the sake of simplicity right now, stick with convention and begin in the east. Walk from the central altar to the eastern part of the Circle (or where you've placed the altar for that direction). Visualize a pure white light filling that space. As you walk the perimeter clockwise, continue visualizing this light shimmering outward, creating a three-dimensional boundary in your mind's eye. Some Witches find it helpful to trace this line with a wand or athame (see Chapter 4) to better direct the energy.

✳ **Wiccan Wonderings: What can be done inside a sacred space once it's created?**

Anything you wish. Read a spiritually inspiring book, meditate, pray, hold a ritual, weave a spell, or work on your Book of Shadows. Within this space, your soul can find a moment of calm and a sense of timelessness. All things are possible—just trust your heart. ◆

As you arrive at each of the four directional points, recite an invocation, welcoming the elemental powers and asking them for protection and support.

This following sample invocation begins in the east and proceeds clockwise around the space. It ends at the center altar with an invocation for Spirit. Note that the elemental energies of each quarter are honored in the words. If symbolic elemental items have been left at these four spots, they should be used somehow during the invocation (for example, lighting a candle to symbolize the presence of that power and to honor it).

East: Beings of Air, Guardians of the East, Breath of Transformation—Come! Be welcome in this sacred space. I/we ask that you stand firm to guard and protect, refresh and motivate. Support the magick created here by conveying my/our wishes on every wind as it reaches across the earth.

South: Beings of Fire, Guardians of the South, Spark of Creation that banishes the darkness—Come! Be welcome in this sacred space. I/we ask that you stand firm to guard and protect, activate and fulfill. Support the magick created here by conveying my/our wishes to the sun, the stars, and every beam of light as it embraces the earth.

West: Beings of Water, Guardians of the West, Rain of Inspiration—Come! Be welcome in this sacred space. I/we ask that you stand firm to guard and protect, heal and nurture. Support the magick created here by conveying my/our wishes to dewdrops and waves as they wash across the world.

North: Beings of Earth, Guardians of the North, Soils of Foundation—Come! Be welcome in this sacred space. I/we ask that you stand firm to guard and protect, mature and provide. Support the magick created here by conveying my/our wishes to every grain of sand, every bit of loam that is our world.

Center: Ancient One . . . the power that binds all the elements into oneness and source of my/our magick—Come! Be welcome in this sacred space. I/we ask that you stand firm to guard and protect, guide and fill all the energy created here. May it be for the good of all. So mote it be.

Releasing the Space

The more you work magick in an area, the more saturated with energy it becomes. Similarly, the more you invoke the quarters in that space, the more protective energy lingers therein. At the end of your workings, release the sphere you've created, thank the powers, ask them to keep guiding the energy you've raised, and bid them farewell until the next time. Breaking the Circle is a symbolic act that signals the completion of your magick. When you break the Circle, the Circle is "opened" and you step back into the ordinary world.

✳ Wiccan Wonderings: What is fire magick?

Fire magick is about enthusiasm, initiative, passion, and energy. Use fire magick when you're feeling lethargic or need to stir up enthusiasm. If you're in need of motivation, fire magick will help you get started. A burner is used when doing this sort of magick. Fire magick also includes candle magick and the magick of the sun (charging a crystal, for example). ✦

Releasing the sacred space is effectively the reverse of erecting it. Begin in the north quarter and move counterclockwise (like you're unwinding something). Instead of envisioning the lines of force forming, see them slowly evaporating back into the void. Just because they leave your sacred space, it doesn't mean they're gone (energy can't be destroyed—it only changes form). They simply return to their source at the four corners of creation and attend to the tasks for which they were made.

As when casting the Circle, add a verbal element to provide closure. Words have very real power. The vibrations they put into the air clarify your understanding of what's happened in the sacred space and elicit evocative images that can dramatically change the outcome of your efforts.

Try this sample invocation for releasing the Circle:

North: Guardians, Guides, and Ancestors of the North and Earth, I/we thank you for your presence and protection. Keep me/us rooted in your rich soil so my/our spirits grow steadily until I/we return to your protection again. Hail and farewell!

West: Guardians, Guides, and Ancestors of the West and Water, I/we thank you for your presence and protection. Keep me/us flowing ever toward wholeness in body, mind, and spirit until I/we return to your protection again. Hail and farewell!

South: Guardians, Guides, and Ancestors of the South and Fire, I/we thank you for your presence and protection. Keep your fires ever burning within my/our soul to light up any darkness and drive it away until I/we return to your protection again. Hail and farewell!

East: Guardians, Guides, and Ancestors of the East and Air. I/we thank you for your presence and protection. Keep your winds blowing fresh with ideas and hopefulness until I/we return to your protection again. Hail and farewell!

Center: Great Spirit, thank you for blessing this space. I/we know that a part of you is always with us, as a still small voice that guides and nurtures. Help me/us to listen to that voice, to trust it, and trust in my/our magick. Merry meet, merry part, and merry meet again.

The Sacred Space of Self

Now and then, there just isn't time to create formalized sacred space. Many Witches overcome this temporal challenge by accepting the idea that each person is a sacred space unto himself or herself. When time is lacking, the clever Witch simply uses visualization (often that of a white-light bubble) to provide herself with sacred sanctuary.

✦ Wiccan Wonderings: What is air magick?

Air magick involves expression and communication. The most powerful air magick you can perform is finding your magick word—the single word that resonates so deeply inside you that you can feel it racing through your bones. Once you find the word, you can use it to focus your personal power during magickal practice, or even to mitigate stress and anxiety anywhere, at any time. Burn incense when doing air magick. ✦

Another alternative is to have four items that symbolize the four elements. Each of these items should be cleansed, blessed, designated for its function, charged, and then placed near its directional point. You can quickly activate a sacred space simply by envisioning the four objects connected by a line of energy, or by offering a shortened invocation and pointing to those spots in the room. Your invocation can be as simple as the following phrase:

> *Earth, Air, Fire, and Water—hear the words of my heart; protection and power impart!*

Bear in mind that abbreviated castings like this can be just as powerful and functional as the long versions, so long as the Witch maintains a respectful demeanor, focus, and intention.

Chapter 4

The Witch's Kit: Tools and Symbolism

NOW THAT YOU KNOW how to find your own sacred space and cast your Circle, it's time to familiarize yourself with some of the tools you'll need for spellcraft. The tools of the Craft speak to our subconscious mind in forms that help support magickal workings. Witches and Wiccans will tell you that tools are good helpmates to magick, but they are not necessary to the success of any spell or ritual. A tool is only a focus, something to distract you from yourself. Without the Witch's will and directed energy, the potential in any tool will remain dormant. For example, a Witch might talk about quartz crystals as having energy-enhancing power, but until a crystal is charged and activated, that ability "sleeps" within. In magick, the Witch is the enabler. A focused will is all that any effective Witch needs for magick. Everything else just makes the job easier.

Athame

The origins of the word *athame* have been lost to history. Some speculate that it may have come from *The Clavicle of Solomon* (published in 1572), which refers to the knife as the *Arthana* (*athame* may be a subverted form of this term). Another theory is that *athame* comes from the Arabic word *al-dhamme* (bloodletter), a sacred knife in the Moorish tradition. In either case, there are magickal manuscripts dating to the

1200s that imply the use of ritual knives in magick (and special knives were certainly used in ancient offerings).

✳ **Wiccan Wonderings: What happens if a specific tool isn't available?**
Find something else with appropriate symbolic value. For instance, some alternatives of an athame include a butter knife or wooden spoon (especially for a Kitchen Witch), a dirk (Scottish Witchcraft), a sword (commonly seen in High Magick), or even a finger. ✦

Modern Wiccans use the knife to represent the male aspect of the Divine and as a symbol of the will (both good and ill). Some Wiccans do not use their knives for anything other than spellcraft and ritual, while others feel that the more they use the tool, the more potent it becomes. There is also a strong belief that an athame used to physically harm another will never again be functional in magick, although in ancient times Witches often "fed" special knives with blood.

Other Alternatives

There are other tools that Witches might use instead of, or in conjunction with, an athame. Some of them include:

Labrys: A double-headed ax that serves as a holy symbol for some Witches, particularly those who choose to follow Artemis or Rhea. The image of a labrys has strong connections with the Greek oracle at Delphi and, as such, is also suitable for anyone following Greek magickal traditions, in combination with or as a substitute for the pentagram (explained later in this chapter).

Staff: An alternative to an athame or wand, used for directing energy. A staff may also be used like a sword in opening energy pathways.

Sword: A High-Magick alternative to an athame. Witches

sometimes use swords to cut an energy pathway into and out of the sacred space once a Circle has been cast.

Wand or rod: These tools have all the functions of an athame. The only difference is that sometimes wands and rods become divinatory tools when carved or painted symbolically and then tossed or cast onto a surface. Some wands, like witching wands (Y-shaped branches), are used to locate lost items or sources of water.

Broom and Cauldron

Modern Witches do not rely on their brooms for flying, nor do they use their cauldrons to make slimy, noxious concoctions. These tools do have a purpose in magickal spells and rituals, however.

Broom (Besom)

The besom is a long-handled tool with a bundle at one end once made from the broom plant, which grows plentifully on European heaths and sandy pastures. Known for its yellow flowers and angular branches, broom is ideal for bundling. Thus, the instrument made of the broom plant and a stick also came to be known as a broom.

The broom is present in the folklore of various countries and cultures. Since Roman times, it has been associated with feminine power and magick. Prior to childbirth, women used a broom to sweep the threshold of a house both for protection and to prepare the way for the new spirit to enter. Gypsy marriage rituals included jumping over a broomstick to ensure the couple's fertility; this ritual neatly marked the line between single and married life.

Cauldron

Wiccans use the cauldron for both symbolic and practical purposes. Cauldrons appear in many mythological accounts; for instance, Odin received wisdom and intuitiveness from a cauldron, and Celtic legend mentions a cauldron of regeneration for the Gods. These types of stories, found in a variety of cultures around the world, give us clues about the origins of the cauldron's modern symbolic value. Specifically, Witches see the cauldron as an emblem of the womb from which all life, and many other gifts, flow. The three-legged cauldron represents the threefold human and divine nature.

⁕ **Wiccan Wonderings: What are cauldrons used for?**
Witches have many practical uses for cauldrons. For example, they may use a cauldron to cook magickal foods and to hold beverages. Additionally, the cauldron can be filled with fire, water, flowers, or other items at specific times of the year to honor the point in the Wheel of the Year that a festival or altar commemorates. ✦

A brazier is a good alternative for a cauldron. *Brazier* comes from a French term meaning "live coals." A brazier is a fire-safe container that can hold a small fire source or burning incense. Braziers are ideal for indoor rituals and spells where fire is a key component.

Other Ritualistic Tools
Additional ritualistic tools commonly used by Witches include aspergers, chalices, goblets, horns, and mirrors.

Asperger: Any item used to sprinkle water in and around the sacred space. In Scotland, a freshly picked branch of heather, which adds a lovely aroma to the water, is often used. Feathers, flowers, leaves, and brooms are all items used for asperging, along with the Witch's handy fingertips!

Chalice or goblet: A symbol of the feminine aspect of the Goddess (and sometimes used to represent the water element). The chalice can be used to make libations. For a symbolic enactment of libations, the Witch places the athame point down in the cup to represent the power of creation that comes from uniting male and female energies.

Horn: An alternative to a cup or goblet, often used among Witches who practice a Norse or Germanic tradition. A horn can also be used as a symbolic item. Place it on the altar during times of need to invoke the spirits of plenty. Musical horns can also be used to call the quarters or to mark the release of a spell (announcing the way for magick).

Mirror: Another multifaceted tool that is usually used in spell-craft to deflect negativity or improve self-image. Mirrors also make wonderful (and handy) scrying surfaces. (Scrying is a type of divination used by Witches.) Mirrors are also commonly used by Witches who blend *feng shui* with their arts.

✦ Wiccan Wonderings: What is water magick?

Use water magick when you need to sharpen your intuition or boost your emotions. The ocean is ideal for water magick when doing love spells. If you don't live near the ocean, incorporate objects from the beach—stones, shells, and sand. Then imagine yourself on a beach somewhere, out in the warm sun. The cup represents water magick when casting spells. Fill your cup with water, wine, or any other liquid you can drink. ✦

Emblems, Costumes, and Regalia

Beyond the basic tools, many Witches have certain personalized emblems and regalia they keep for specific spells and rituals.

Cords: In addition to holding robes in place, cords can also indicate a Witch's level of skill in a specific tradition or group. Exactly how this custom came into being is uncertain. It may connect with the umbilical cord, thereby symbolizing a Witch's connection to the Sacred Parent, or perhaps even the myth of Ariadne's thread leading Theseus safely out of the labyrinth (which is a metaphor for life). Historically, cords were used in spellcraft, especially knot magick in

Egypt, Arabia, and Europe, and they continue to carry that role today.

Crosses: An equidistant cross represents crossroads (an in-between place), the four corners of creation, the elemental powers, and the four quarters of the Sacred Circle. Some Witches prefer to wear the cross in lieu of a pentagram.

Crystals, metals, minerals, and shells: Nearly all types of crystals, gems, metals, minerals, and shells have been categorized for their elemental and magickal correspondences. Many Witches keep crystals on their altars to generate or collect specific types of energy, carry stones as amulets and charms, and even make crystal elixirs to internalize a specific stone's attributes.

✦ **Wiccan Wondering: What are Sigils?**

Sigils are used for various purposes, such as astrological emblems or symbols for the Gods and Goddesses. In Witchcraft, they function similarly to runes. ✦

Masks play a role in sympathetic magick, whereby a person "becomes" what the item represents in the sacred space. This provides an extrasensory dimension in ritual and helps improve the overall result.

Pentagram: A symbol worn by many Witches to represent the harmony of the elements, Spirit, and the self working together to create magick. The pentagram is also sometimes employed as a protective ward in written form either on paper or on the floor of a ritual space. Without the Circle around it, the pentagram is known as a pentacle, Solomon's Seal, and the Witch's cross.

Poppets: Typically, poppets are created in the image of a specific person or creature so sympathetic magick can be directed from a distance at the subject represented. (Poppets can also represent a situation.) For instance, if you were to make a poppet of a beloved pet and carefully wrap it in white cloth to protect it, the animal would then receive the benefit of that protection. Witches also use corn or wheat to make poppets that represent the "spirit" of the grain, and keep them at home to ensure luck, a good harvest, and ongoing protection. Since the maker has a strong emotional bond to the poppet and uses that bond to affect a person over a long distance, the poppet qualifies as a talisman as well (see Chapter 5 for information on talismans).

Robes: While some Witches practice skyclad (naked), robes and other accoutrements help Witches to "dress for the occasion" by separating that particular time from everyday-life events. Additionally, many covens use special markings or colors to indicate different things, like the season or a person's level of achievement in the group.

Key Ingredients for Spells

It's reasonably safe to say that there is not a stone, plant, animal, or other natural item that hasn't been used at one time or another for magickal purposes, especially spellcraft. As any good cook will tell you, the key to great food lies in the ingredients and how they are combined. The same thing is true for spells. If you think of a spell as a magickal recipe, you will begin to understand why the components (that is, the ingredients) are so important. If the components are not measured correctly, if they are not added to the mix at the right time, if you don't give them enough time to "bake" properly, the magick goes awry. The magickal ingredients give flavor to the magick, and that has been the case throughout history.

So what constitutes a good spell component? Anything that's essential to the recipe—anything that builds the energy until it's just right. It's important for all the ingredients to mesh on a metaphysical level. Their energy needs both continuity and congruity. Of course, the Witch herself can be the key component of any spell, with but a word, a touch, or a wish!

✳ Wiccan Wonderings: How do Witches view nature?

Gifts from nature are among the most highly prized tools in Wicca and Witchcraft. Since Witches believe that through creation, they can eventually come to know the Creator better, it's not surprising that they study nature and apply its symbolic value to their Craft. ✦

The lists that follow are by no means comprehensive, but provide enough information so that you can eventually design your own spells. You don't need to run out and buy everything on these lists; select a few staples that seem to fit the kinds of spells you're interested in casting. As you become more proficient with spells, you'll compile your own lists of what works and what doesn't.

Aromatic Oils

Our sense of smell is so acutely connected to memory that a single scent can conjure virtually any detail and instantly take you back to various phases of your life. All it takes is the whiff of a certain perfume, of sea air, or of fresh baked apple pie and a slew of memories surrounding the person who is, or was, the love of your life instantly ensues. So it's no surprise that aromatic oils are used rather extensively in love spells.

Following is a list of essential oils. These oils aren't to be ingested. They are best used in aromatherapy burners or in ritual baths. When anointing a candle with an oil, as some spells call for, rub upward from the base toward the top of the candle.

Acacia: meditation, purification
Almond: vitality, energy booster
Basil: harmony
Bay: good for love spells, prophetic dreams

Bayberry: money spells

Cedar: instills courage; good for protection, money, prosperity

Clove: healing, love spells, increases sexual desire

Eucalyptus: healing

Frankincense: prosperity, protection, psychic awareness

Honeysuckle: mental clarity, money

Jasmine: love spells, meditation, to sweeten any situation

Lavender: healing, purification, love spells

Mint: money spells

Patchouli: love spells, protection, money spells

Rue: protection

Sage: cleansing, wisdom

Vervain: money spells, fertility

Ylang-ylang: aphrodisiac, love spells, increases sexual desire

Herbs

In addition to a stash of essential oils, you'll want to stock up on essential herbs as well.

Acacia: for meditation; to ward off evil; to attract money and love

Angelica: for temperance; to guard against evil

Anise: for protection: The seeds can be burned as a meditation incense; the scent of the fruit awakens energies needed in magickal practices.

Balm: soothes emotional pain; mitigates fears

Basil: balance, money, purification, divination

Bay: heals; purifies; good for divination, psychic development, and awareness

Burdock: purifies and cleanses; protection; psychic awareness; wards off negativity; aphrodisiac

Catnip: insight, love, happiness

Chamomile: to bless a person, thing, or place; for meditation; also a sleep aid; helps attract money

Cinnamon: good for love spells, purification

Cinquefoil: energy; memory stimulator; allows you to speak your mind; protection; eloquence in speech; also aids in divination, healing, psychic dreams

Clove: to get rid of negativity; cleansing

Clover: heightens psychic awareness; love spells, luck

Daisy: attracts good luck; love divinations

Elder: protection, healing rituals

Foxglove: heightens sexuality

Frankincense: meditation, power, psychic visions; used mainly as incense

Garlic: personal protection; healing; to lift depression

Ginger: love, assistance for quick manifestation

Hawthorne: success, happiness, fertility, protection

Jasmine: peace, harmony; to sweeten a situation or person, attract money, induce prophetic dreams

Kava-kava: heightens psychic awareness; good luck; anti-anxiety

Laurel: for attaining success and victory

Lavender: healing, spiritual and psychic development, love spells

Mandrake: toxic, handle with care, do not burn or inhale— used in amulets for luck, protection, fertility; many ancient mystical properties

Marigold: love, healing, psychic awareness, marriage spells, success in legal matters

Marjoram: acceptance of major life changes

Mint: speeds up results in a spell; prosperity and healing; attracts money

Mugwort: as a tea, aids in divination, psychic development and awareness, and meditation; good for washing crystals

Myrrh: usually burned with frankincense for protection, healing, consecration

Nettle: mitigates thorny situations such as gossip and envy

Parsley: protection, calming effect, eases money problems, good for health spells

Rosemary: protection, love, health; improves memory

Rue: strengthens willpower; good for health; speeds recovery from illness and surgery; expels negativity

Sage: excellent for cleansing a place with negative vibes; protection, wisdom, mental clarity; attracts money

Sandalwood: protection, spiritual communication, conjuring of good spirits, healing

Skullcap: relaxation before magickal practices

Thyme: helps to focus energy and is used to prepare oneself for magickal practice

Vervain: a favorite herb of the Druids; cleanses negative vibes; good for protection, general boost to the spirit; attracts riches; good for creativity, divination; used as an aphrodisiac

Willow: love, protection, conjuring of spirits, healing

Wormwood: poisonous if burned—facilitates spirit communication; good for love charms; enhances psychic ability

Yarrow: divination, love, protection; enhances psychic ability

Incense

Incense has numerous functions for Witches. First, specially prepared blends like cedar and myrrh clear the air of any unwanted energies. Second, the smoke carries wishes and prayers to the winds (in this case, the aromatic base should match the intention of the wish). Third, burning incense can represent either the fire or air element in the sacred space.

It isn't very hard to make homemade incense. Just grind up some aromatic wood using a pencil sharpener that's been cleaned out; then add some finely powdered kitchen herbs or dried flowers. This incense requires a fire source to burn, but it works very nicely.

Colors and Candles

Unless you're color blind, color is intrinsic to your world. Yet, most of us take colors for granted—until we take a moment to appreciate a particularly stunning sunset, or marvel at the vivid hues in a painting.

Science has proven that colors have a particular vibration, a tone that touches us in a particular way. Blues, pale greens, and pinks are tranquil; that's why you find them in hospitals, waiting rooms, and the dentist's office. Red stimulates and energizes; that's why your favorite Chinese restaurant is predominantly red. Yellow and gold buoy our spirits.

The colors you use in casting spells are a vital ingredient in the power of the spell. Even if you know nothing about color or spells, you probably wouldn't use black to attract money because you intuitively know that green or gold fit much better when trying to attract prosperity, money, and abundance. Likewise, it isn't much of a stretch to figure out that pink represents love and red represents passion. You can incorporate particular colors into your spells when using cloths to cover your altar, quartz crystals, stones and gems, or candles.

✦ Wiccan Wonderings: Which types of items can be charged?

You can charge the oils you use in spells just as you would a crystal or stone. Place your bottle of oil in the windowsill where light will spill over it. You can request particular things from the oil, or just say a general prayer. Let it charge for an hour, then use it. If you live near an ocean and find shells that are whole and nearly perfect, you can also charge these power objects by washing them in salt water and putting them out into the sun for a while. ✦

Candles, in fact, are an essential ingredient in many spells. They can be used as either the focus of the spell or as a component that sets the spell's overall mood and tone. When imbued with personal power, they provide a means for focusing attention, and they offer protection. Lighting a candle represents igniting energy; carving a candle indicates the intention of the user; and pinning a candle marks the melting spot at which the magick will be released (kind of like an X marking the spot on a treasure map).

The symbolic value of the candle goes further. The flame represents the element of fire, which in turn signifies inspiration, passion, energy, and cleansing. Spells that require a fire source as a focus or component can easily be cast with a candle instead of a full-blown bonfire.

In various ritual constructs, candles represent the individual's soul, the presence of Spirit, or any one of the elemental powers. Candles may also be used for scrying, as a spell focus or component, and as a way of shifting the overall ambiance of an area to something more magickal.

No matter the application, Witches will often choose the candle's color and aroma to match the theme of the magick being created. For example, a simple white candle adorns the altar to represent purity of Spirit.

It's best to have candles in a variety of colors. The list below gives the basic meanings of colors used in spells.

Amber: psychic sensitivity

Black: removing hexes, protection, spirit contact and communication

Blue: element of water, dreams, protection, intuition, health

Brown: element of earth, physical objects, perseverance

Gold: success, power, prosperity, healing energy, higher intuition

Green: element of earth, lady luck, healing, balance, money

Lavender: spiritual and psychic development, divination, mediumship

Orange: balance, clearing the mind, healing, attracting what you need or want

Pink: health, love, friends

Purple: spiritual power and development, business matters, spiritual wisdom

Red: element of fire, passion and sexuality, energy, courage, enthusiasm

Silver: psychic development, beginnings, intuition, meditation

Violet: psychic development and awareness, intuition

White: understanding, clarity, peace, protection, truth

Yellow: element of air, contracts, divination, mental clarity, creativity

Gemstones and Crystals

Stones have a long history in the practice of magick. Gems appeared on sacred altars across the world as offerings to the divinities, and they cropped up in global superstitions with a multitude of virtuous powers. Gems could heal, protect, inspire fertility, indicate the outcome of battles, and improve crop growth. Some historians and folklorists have even raised the possibility that the original intent for wearing jewelry was more strongly based on the talismanic quality of its gems than as mere decoration. In the distant past, crystals were just as valuable as gems, simply because of their gemlike qualities and their scarcity. Today, crystals are far less costly and much more available than gems.

Stones and crystals are generally used when you want or need to affect the deeper layers of reality. Like herbs and colors, each stone has a different magickal property. Just as a sculptor releases the form inherent in a stone, so does the magickal practitioner release the power of a particular stone. With the proper attitude, a piece of jade will work as well as an emerald.

The relationship you have with your stones will be unique to you. Some will feel exactly right for whatever issue or purpose you have in mind; others won't "speak" to you at all. If you're going to work with stones, try reading a book called *Gemisphere Luminary* by Michael Katz. Each chapter discusses a particular stone and covers its history, spiritual properties, and role in the evolving consciousness of man.

✳ **Wiccan Wonderings: What's the best way to store stones used for spells?**

Some people recommend keeping stones in a velvet or cloth bag, a wooden box, or a special place, and they warn against other people touching them. Somehow, though, this seems old-fashioned and superstitious. It's fine to keep your stones where they can be seen, touched, and enjoyed. Just cleanse them with salt water and let them sit in the sunlight for a while before you use them for a particular purpose, in order to charge them. ✦

The guidelines provided below for stones and their magickal properties are simply a place to begin. With time, you'll develop your own ideas about which stones to use for which spells.

Agate: Those that look like eyes were used to protect from the evil eye curse (and can still be used for protective magick).

Amber: Lore tells us that amber came from the tears of a setting sun, and as such it's still used as a solar/fire stone. Witches also use it in healing magick (to capture disease much as it did insects).

Amethyst: A spiritual stone. It can be used for meditation, for enhancing and remembering dreams, for cultivating wisdom, for the development of psychic ability, to attract success and prosperity. Also helps with self-control, business cunning, courage, and safety in battle. It ranges in color from deep purple to rose.

Apache tears: This is a type of obsidian that many Witches carry for luck.

Aquamarine: A gift of the sea Goddess, this stone bears the power of the Full Moon and helps manifest harmony, bravery, intuitive awareness, clarity, and a stronger connection with our superconscious. It is also good for healing, aids in the creative process, awakens spirituality, and fosters awareness of other levels of reality.

Azurite: The blue color of this crystal makes it ideal for dream magick and overall harmony.

Beryl: A transparent to translucent glassy mineral, beryl is used to promote harmony in relationships, success with legal issues, and motivation. Transparent varieties of beryl in white, green, pink, blue, and yellow are valued as gems.

Bloodstone: Healing, to connect more deeply with planetary energy. Also used for wish fulfillment, success, understanding weather omens, safeguarding health. Especially lucky for those born under the astrological sign of Pisces.

Carbuncle: Blood red in color, legend tells that carbuncles forms from the eyes of dragons. Its magickal correspondences include insight, health, and intuitiveness.

Calcite: Comes in a lot of colors, giving it a variety of potential magickal applications. Its energy is suited to encouraging spiritual growth, inner healing, and improved focus.

Cat's eye: The visual impact of this stone gives it strong associations with vision, especially our inner sight. Superstition tells us that cat's eye manifests beauty, luck, and prosperity.

Chalcedony: Offers protection from evil, good fortune, improved communication and attitudes. According to legend, Mohammed wore a ring with this stone set in it. Carnelian, a pale-to-deep or brownish red variety of chalcedony, provides extra protection.

Chrysocolla: This opaque, charcoal-colored stone banishes fear and re-establishes logical perspectives.

Citrine: A pale yellow variety of crystalline quartz, citrine is a great stone for banishing nightmares and improving psychic abilities.

Diamond: Bravery, strength, invulnerability, clarity, and devotion. Among Hindus, Arabs, and Persians, the diamond represents overall success. Lore recounts how diamonds were formed by a thunderbolt.

Emerald: Clairvoyance and divination, healing, growth. The emerald supports magick for faith, foreknowledge, strengthening the conscious mind, and resourcefulness. When emerald is worn with aventurine, another green stone, the two supposedly work synergistically to rid the body of cancer.

Flourite: This crystalline stone seems to strengthen the conscious mind and thinking skills.

Garnet: This gem was used in the Middle Ages to protect the bearer from nightmares. Witches use garnet for devotion, good health, and kindness. Nongemstone quality garnet is also available.

Jade: Jade has long been used as an amulet to encourage prosperity, enhance beauty, and inspire harmony, love, longevity, and the proverbial "green thumb" for those with poor luck in gardening. Low-quality jade is widely available.

Jasper: Used by the Ancient Egyptians, red jasper is good for love spells and to stir up passions. Brown jasper is excellent for healing purposes. The stone also comes in yellow and green, but is most often found in the reddish hues and with mixed, swirling colors throughout its surface.

Lapis lazuli: For opening psychic channels, improving magickal insights, happiness, and meditative focus, dealing with children, and stimulating the upper chakras. Some of the best lapis comes from Chile, where it's inexpensive and often carved into animal figures. Shamans there use it in their spiritual practices. The most coveted lapis is a deep bluish hue, with almost no white flecks in it.

Malachite: A light to dark greenish stone, malachite can be attached to a child's crib to improve sleep or carried for protection, specifically to remain aware of any forthcoming dangers or problems.

Moldavite: Energizes psychic talent, quickens spiritual evolution. Although not necessarily used in magickal practices, many people who wear it claim it affects them in a positive manner. (Make sure to wear it hanging about level with your heart.)

Moldavite is regarded as an extraterrestrial stone because it resulted from a meteor collision with the earth nearly 15 million years ago. It fell over the Moldau River valley in the Czech Republic. Legend says that moldavite was the green stone in the Holy Grail.

Moonstone: Under the rule of the moon, this stone bears very similar energy to the lunar sphere. Use magickally to motivate foresight, psychism, inventiveness, and nurturing abilities, and to enhance the vividness of dreams and dream recall. Great for Cancerian individuals.

Obsidian: One of the favorite stones for scrying mirrors, and sacred to the patroness of Witches, Hecate.

Onyx: For banishing and absorbing negative energy. Good for grounding during magickal work. Helps to break deeply ingrained habits, whether physical or emotional. Wear onyx when facing adversaries in figurative or literal battle.

Opal: For those born in October, opal is a luck stone that improves memory.

Pearl: Pearls are sacred to Isis in Egypt and Freya among the Saxons, they are also a symbol of the Goddess, the moon, and the water element. Pearls are suited to spells focused on love, happiness, and prosperity.

Peridot (chrysolite): When set in gold, this gem turns away evil, nightmares, and malevolent magick.

Quartz: An all-purpose magickal stone, quartz represents infinite potential. The color of the quartz often varies its applications (for instance, use rosy quartz for friendship and love magick).

Rose quartz: For healing and balance, and to amplify psychic energy. In magickal practices, quartz is often used in conjunction with other stones or orbs for a particular effect.

Ruby: Considered the most excellent amulet for health, mental clarity, and harmony. Also stimulates the emotions, passion, unconditional love.

Sapphire: Brings divine blessings, the ability to understand omens and signs, luck, success, improved meditative states, and devotion.

Tiger's eye: Self-confidence, the freedom to follow your own path. In Rome, soldiers carried these into battle for safety. In modern times, this yellowish-brown stone appears in spells and rituals aimed at improved stamina, good fortune, and prosperity.

Tourmaline: While this stone has little in the way of known ancient usage, it comes in a variety of colors, offering Witches flexibility in its applications. Overall, tourmaline seems to balance energy.

Turquoise: Safety in travel, rain magick, visual acuity, strength in friendship, and improved awareness.

This is just a brief list of stones. Many others are used in magickal work and, over time, you can compile your own personal list as you learn which ones work best for particular spells.

✦ Wiccan Wonderings: What is earth magick?

Earth magick is great for money and prosperity spells. It's also about nature. If you're in need of earth magick, go camping, hiking, or get out into the air and appreciate the natural beauty that surrounds you. The bowl that represents earth magick is often filled with rice, but you can fill your bowl with any food that is grown. ✦

Metals and Minerals

A good portion of the correspondences for metals and minerals comes to us through alchemists, the medieval chemists who searched for gold and instead discovered many other substances and their properties. Alchemists believed that everything on this planet could be broken down into key elemental correspondences; they often worked during the Waxing Moon to improve the results of their studies. Take a look at the following list of metals and minerals to familiarize yourself with their magickal correspondences and traits.

Boji stone: A projective stone Witches use to inspire symmetry, peacefulness, and a sense of foundation.

Brass: Brass is a fire-oriented metal that exhibits energy similar to gold but on a gentler scale. It's popular in healing and prosperity magick.

Copper: The preferred metal for making witching wands, copper conducts energy and inspires health, balance, and good foundations.

Feldspar: This substance is made of aluminum silicate and other minerals. Egyptians used feldspar as a tonic for headaches and other minor ailments. Magickally, it's associated with love, fertility, and working with the fey.

Flint: Durability; protection from mischievous fairies.

Gold: The metal of the sun and the God aspect, gold confers strength, leadership, power, authority, and victory to the bearer.

Hematite: Pliny recommended this iron ore to attract positive energy and exude charm. The ancient writers put hematite under the rule of Mars, which would also give it the powers of protection and strength.

Iron: Strength, safety, protection from spirits. Some consider iron an antimagick metal, which is why Witches prefer not to cut magickal herbs with an iron knife.

Lead: Greeks inscribed pieces of lead with incantations and then used them as amulets to ward against negative charms and spells. Its weight provides it with symbolism for reconnecting to the earth (keeping one foot on the ground), having a firm anchor, and overall practicality.

Lodestone: The magnetic quality of this stone makes it ideal for attracting overall good vibrations into the Witch's life. In particular, it's good for relationship magick.

Meteorites: Because they come from celestial realms, meteorites are good for meditation, and for directing your attention to your place in the greater scheme of things. Promotes astral projection and improves understanding of universal patterns.

Pyrite: Carry this to protect yourself from being fooled.

Salt: At one time this substance was so valued as to be used as currency (Rome). Today Witches use salt or salt water for consecrating items or the sacred space, for banishing, and overall protective energies.

Serpentine: A greenish, brownish, or spotted mineral used as a protective stone, mostly health-oriented.

Silver: The metal of the moon and the Goddess, silver inspires insight, dreams, psychic awareness, and creativity.

Steel: Steel is typically used to protect the bearer from fairies, or to afford general protection (especially when made into a ring).

Tin: A lucky metal, especially if you put it in your shoe.

Plain Stones, Shells, and Fossils

In addition to gems, crystals, and minerals, there are other stones and stonelike objects that people have used in magick, and that modern Witches and Wiccans continue to use. Each carries a specific energy imprint that the Witch activates and directs for specific goals.

Coral: Red and pink coral are the preferred types for protecting children. Carry coral for wisdom, insight, and to connect with the water element or lunar energies.

Cross stone: Sometimes called a fairy cross, this is a gifting stone that (because of its shape) honors the four quarters and their corresponding elements.

Geode: The geode has the power to create a natural womb for energy, and is an ideal Goddess emblem.

Hag stone: Also known as a holey stone, it's a plain rock found near the water that has a hole going all the way through it. This stone stimulates health, luck, and blessings, and is considered the gift of the sea Goddess.

Jet: This ancient fossilized bit of wood provides strength and courage, particularly in difficult situations.

Lava: Being born of fire, lava burns away sickness and negativity.

Petrified wood: If you can determine the tree from which a piece comes, this fossil's energies will be connected to that type of tree. More generically, petrified wood helps you honor cycles in your life and improves the longevity of beloved projects.

Pumice: This is a very light stone. Carry a piece of pumice when you wish to ease your burdens and make the road ahead a little less difficult.

Round stone: To discover a perfectly round stone is considered good fortune, so if you find one, keep it. It also represents the Sacred Circle.

Sand dollar: A gift from the sea, the sand dollar provides protective energy, especially of your personal resources and energies (note the natural pentagram design).

Shells: Another gift from the sea, shells help us reconnect with the ancient ocean mother. They're good charms for improving divinatory ability, for learning to "go with the flow," and for acquiring the ability to listen to the voice of Spirit.

Stalagmites and stalactites: Once carried for protection and male fertility, stalagmites produce upward moving energy, while stalactites move downward. Stalagmites and stalactites may be used as magickal symbols of increasing or banishing power, respectively.

White stone: Among the Celts, a white stone found adjacent to a holy well could help the bearer see fairies.

Chapter 5

Spellcraft Fundamentals

LOOKING BACK OVER the legacy of Witchcraft, spells have always been the primary technique in the Witch's kit, perhaps because they are an easily accessible form of magick. Some spells need nothing more than the Witch's presence to manifest power. This chapter will introduce you to some of the most popular forms of spellcraft used throughout the ages and in today's community. Although the chief ingredients or words used in spells might have changed depending on the culture and social climate, the basic processes have not. This is wonderful for the Witch who looks to tradition or who simply wants to honor history in her practices.

Don't think that respecting tradition limits the modern Witch, though. A lot of people who are new to magick often ask if it's okay to create their own spells. The answer is a resounding yes. After all, someone, somewhere had to come up with the first spell, and hundreds of thousands of spells have been created after that! Personally created spells are a birthright and often considered a very important step in the Witch's training and adeptness.

It would be difficult in a book of this size to impart a comprehensive overview of spells and their origins. It is possible, however, to put spellcraft into perspective by relaying snippets of history and sharing spells from hundreds of years ago that are still used today.

Sympathy and the Law of Similars

To understand how spells work, it is necessary to understand sympathy and the Law of Similars. Sympathy basically means that a symbolic item, when properly used, has the power to act on something or someone by virtue of its sympathetic relation. For example, to heal a cut made by a dagger, put salve on the dagger—it will help to heal the wound caused by it, due to the relationship between the wound, the dagger, and your action. This technique would also help to prevent similar wounds from happening again because you're effectively "forgiving" the dagger for cutting you.

The Law of Similars is a little different. According to this law, there is a divine fingerprint in nature, one that gives clues to an item's spiritual function. For example, red plants might be used in magickal cures for blood problems, and a heart-shaped leaf might be part of a love spell. Poppets (described in Chapter 4) were designed with the concept of sympathy and the Law of Similars in mind. The Egyptians were the first to use them in spellcraft, making the dolls very carefully, dressing them, and adding incantations that designated the poppet's desired effect on the person it represented.

Thousands of years later, scientists who study subliminal perception have confirmed those practices. Today, figurative representations play a part in everything from advertising to religion, affecting the subconscious in specific ways. Witches certainly aren't left out of this picture. You can still find many spells that employ an item's shape as part of the overall meaning, like using a phallus-shaped stone in a spell for male virility. In this manner, Witches believe they are giving greater dimension to the energy a spell creates, so it will manifest more specifically.

A Blessing Look, a Healing Touch

Although this theory has no proof, some believe that physically oriented spells were probably among the first to develop. Because so much symbolic value was ascribed to various parts of the human body, the mental connection needed to make the magick work was already in place.

Eyes are the windows of the soul. Feet hold up the body and transport it, offer great stability, but also have the power to kick and crush things. Our hands serve, heal, build, welcome, support, offer aid, and fulfill a million other responsibilities. You might have noticed that priests and priestesses around the world maintain eye contact with the people they serve and often use their hands in blessing, even to this day. This approach creates a very real bond and helps energy flow more freely from one person to another. The Witch's methods are really no different.

The following list contains some examples of physically oriented spells:

Banishing: To rid herself of an enemy, the Witch may stomp out that person's path through the woods, symbolically taking power over that person's very footsteps.

Enchantment: Trying to charm another person or object might include a long "come hither" look as part of the process or the whole of the spell in order to weave the desired person into the magick.

Healing: Nearly all healing spells employ hand motion and touching the patient. In modern times, people have learned much about the importance of touch, which gives this approach even more merit.

Knots of Good Luck

A knot can be made from just about anything, and the symbolic value of binding or releasing certainly wasn't lost on our ancestors. Knot magick most likely originated with the arts of weaving, sewing, and fishing, all three of which use knotting in one form or another. A woman weaving her husband a scarf would bind a little magick into every strand to protect his health. A fisherman would tie knots in his fishing net to attract a better catch. (A seafaring fisherman might also knot a rope and hang it from his sail. When winds weren't favorable, releasing one knot would also release a light wind to take the boat where it needed to go.)

✳ Wiccan Wonderings: Are complicated spells more powerful than simpler ones?
Magick doesn't have to be complicated to work. Complexity doesn't imply power, nor does simplicity mean weak magickal results. If anything, the simpler the better. It gives you more time to focus your mind and spirit on the task at hand. ✦

Though knot magick developed independently in different cultures throughout history, there were generally two common elements. First is the use of numeric symbolism in the knot spell, for example, tying a money knot four times (four is an "earth" number associated with prosperity). Second is the binding of specific energy into each knot with incantations or symbolic objects. For instance, if a fisherman wanted to attract fish, he or she might bind a small piece of bait into the net and release the knot as the net was lowered.

Modern Wiccans and Witches still use knot symbolism in the following types of spells:

- Bindings and banishings (especially of illness and negative energy)
- Channeling energy into a specific location (energy can be captured in the knot, then released when needed)
- Fixing relationships
- "Tying up the loose ends" of a situation

A Witch may choose to create lines of knots (akin to a rosary) for specific functions and keep them in a safe place (like on the altar) for use as needed. These lines are sometimes called a Witch's Ladder.

Untying one knot represents the release of the energy bound therein and the beginning of a particular spell. Alternatively, if a Witch or Wiccan notices that there is a problem with unwanted energies in a space, he or she may quickly tie a knot in a piece of clothing or the altar cloth to constrain that problem until after the magickal working.

Portable Magick

Charms, amulets, fetishes, talismans, and other types of portable magick comprise a huge portion of the Witch's kit. In times when people travel both short and long distances without a second thought, these types of accessible items are becoming even more important. Taking spellcraft on the road has never been easier.

In modern vernacular, the words charm, amulet, and talisman are often used interchangeably. From a historical perspective, however, they were not the same. To honor tradition and begin understanding what makes each process unique, it's important to define the terms. In brief, the main differences are derived from the way the energy in each is eventually applied; whether the tokens are active or passive in nature; and the manner in which each was created.

Charms

Although the term *charm* has come to be applied to small symbolic items that are carried to encourage good fortune or avert evil, charms (verbal spells) were originally nothing more than sacred words uttered with intention. These were probably the first and easiest form of portable magick in ancient spellcraft. Most likely this had a lot to do with linguistics. A variety of magickal processes, which seem to appear later in history than charms (like the making of talismans and fetishes), use words that link them back to charms. This approach makes sense if you consider that a wise Witch realizes he can always rely on his voice, his gift of speech. This convenient form of spellcraft certainly does go with you everywhere.

The word *charm* comes from a Latin term, *carmen*, which means "incantation" or "song." A charm is like a poem—many charms rhyme or have a distinct rhythm in their delivery, making it easier for the Witch to commit them to memory—no need to carry a huge Grimoire around, no scrolls to get damaged in the rain en route to market!

✳ Wiccan Wonderings: How long do charms last?

Charms remain active once they have been created (unless the Witch intended otherwise), and typically, their energy lasts less than a year. ✦

Besides rhyme and meter, charms incorporate other magickal ideas in their mechanisms. For example, a Witch might wait until the first night of a Full Moon to recite the charm, then recite it thrice each night thereafter. The Full Moon represents "fullness," coming to manifestation, and the intuitive mind. The number three represents the body-mind-spirit connection or the triune nature of many of the world's divine figures. In this manner, the Witch combines lyrical verse with other symbolic systems to improve the results of the charm.

The following example is a simple verbal charm from Europe:

Leaf of ash,
I do thee pluck
To bring to me
A day of luck.

This charm isn't a literary masterpiece, and yours don't have to be either. What's important is that the charm expresses your wish or goal, and that it's easy to remember. That way, you can repeat it whenever it comes to mind, giving the original charm more energy to work toward manifestation.

It's quite common for charms to be repeated a specific number of times. This repetition gives the charm a musical attribute and wraps it in the Witch's will. The other reason for repetition is the mystical value of numbers. To add this dimension to this charm, for example, a practitioner might repeat the phrase a certain number of times—for example, eight times (the manifestation number), or twelve times (the number that represents cycles coming to fruition).

In the example above, the spoken charm can be easily followed by a physical charm. As the Witch speaks the word "pluck," she takes the leaf from the ash tree, which she carries all day to inspire good fortune. Many physical charms are derived from nature; a four-leaf clover or a rabbit's foot are good examples. They already bear symbolic value and inherent power that simply needs to be activated by the carrier (often by using a verbal charm to empower it).

During the nineteenth century, manmade charms also became more popular, specifically in the form of charm bracelets, often given as presents. Each charm had meaning and its own special blessings for the recipient. An anchor represented strong foundations; a heart was the gift of love; and a flower charm conferred health.

Written Spells

In the past, many wise people were more literate than the rest of the populace; written spellcraft followed on the heels of verbal charms. Words have power, and the written word in many cultures was revered as a gift of the Gods, especially among the Egyptians and Greeks. With this in mind, it's no surprise that written spellcraft came to be considered more potent than verbal forms.

Written spells relied on the methods used for making charms. They might be timed by auspicious astrological conjunction or be written a set number of times. With written magick, the word's meaning, the color of the ink, the shape of the paper, and even aromatics added to the ink or paper contribute to the overall effect of the spell. Why go through all this fuss? Because Witches believe that the more dimensions magick has (with sensual dimensions being especially significant), the better the results will be.

✳ Wiccan Wonderings: What is low magick?

Low magick commonly focuses its efforts on everyday needs. A charm, for example, is considered a "low" form of magick, no matter the extra frills, because it is not something highly ritualized. When practicing your spellcraft, remember the kind of clever improvisation found in charms and other forms of low magick. ◆

The words in written charms must reflect the goal of the magick by their meaning and by either the way they are written or what happens to them afterward. For instance, if you're trying to banish a habit, you might write the name of that habit backward on paper, or write it on the paper and then burn it so that it disappears!

One of the oldest, and most well-known written spells is the Gnostic spell that uses Abracadabra (no, we're not pulling a rabbit out of a hat). In the original Chaldean texts, Abracadabra translates as "to perish like the word," and it was customarily used to banish sickness. The process was relatively simple. Abracadabra was written in the form of a descending triangle on parchment, which was then laid on the inflicted body part. Then the paper was stuck in the cleft of a tree and left there so that as time and the elements destroyed the paper, the magick would begin its work.

Amulets

Unlike charms, amulets are passive until something external creates a need for their energy; therefore, their energy tends to last longer. An amulet's main purpose is protection; specifically, it wards off unwanted magick or other baneful influences like lightning and thievery. In some cases, amulets were contrived for purposes similar to charms, such as improving strength, increasing personal wealth, and augmenting magickal power. The word amulet comes from Latin *amuletum*, which means (you guessed it) "a charm"! It's no wonder people still confuse one with the other.

The Greeks called amulets *amylon*, or "food." This definition implies that people used food offerings to ask Gods and Goddesses for protection (and might have even eaten or carried a small bit of that food as an amuletic token).

Many items found in the natural world have been used to fashion amulets. Nearly every type of plant has been used at one time or another. Carved stone and metal are also used, and the more precious the base material, the better the amulet is thought to work. Animals were chosen for their qualities so those qualities could be transferred to the bearer of the properly prepared amulet. For example, wearing an amulet formed out of lion skin would offset fear when the bearer was in battle or on the hunt.

✦ **Wiccan Wonderings: Must amulets always be carried?**
Not necessarily. They can be worn, placed with valuable items, put on pet collars, hung in windows, planted in gardens, or put anywhere else their protective and safeguarding energy is desired. ✦

Amulets were also commonly chosen for their shape or where they were found. For example, Europeans often carried a holey stone (any stone with a hole going through it) to ward off malicious fairies (which would be trapped in the hole). A crystal found adjacent to a sacred well, known for its healthful qualities, would be carried as an amulet to protect the bearer's well-being. In this regard, amulets and charms have a lot in common.

The major difference between making charms and amulets is that the ancient magi were very precise in their instructions on how to make amulets. The base components had to be organized and measured precisely, and any carvings had to be done in an exact order. Say, for example, a Witch wanted to create a health amulet for a sickly person. Copper would be a good base material. An emblem for recovery would be applied to the copper base first, since that was the

Amulets Around the World

A good example of a readily recognized amulet in Western tradition is the horseshoe placed over a doorway. To work properly, the horseshoe must be found rather than taken from an animal. Some people mount it upward to catch any negativity, while others mount it downward so it can rain blessings on everyone who enters.

Amulets in other cultures include:

Brass ring (Lapland): Worn on the right arm to keep ghosts away.
God figurines (Assyria): Buried near the home to protect all within.
Lapis lazuli eyes (Egypt): Placed in tombs to safeguard the soul's journey.
Metal rattles (Ancient Rome): Tied to children's clothing for overall protection.
Miniature carved canoe (Iroquois): Protection from drowning.
Monkey teeth (Borneo): For strength and skill.
Peach stone (China): General ward against evil.
Spruce needles (Shoshone): Keep sickness at bay.

primary necessity. Afterward, a symbol for ongoing protection from sickness would be added. It was (and still is) customary for the practitioner to recite charms over the amulet as it was created.

Talismans

Talismans are also used as active participants in magick. The Witch's wand is a good example of how a talisman operates because it transports energy and helps in casting spells. A Wand is a talisman of power (akin to the Rod of Moses). Many old stories tell us that talismans had indwelling spirits that were commanded by the magick user to do specific tasks. Instances of this nature are rare today, and the word *talisman* is now used to refer to any token that has been created during auspicious astrological times with the right materials.

Like amulets, for talismans to function properly the appropriate materials must be used. For example, when making a talisman to prevent drunkenness, amethyst is an ideal base component because it helps with self-control. To this base all manner of other methods and materials may be added. It is especially important to create the item at a specific time and recite incantations over it.

Traditional Talismans

Aladdin's lamp was a kind of talisman. The lamp held a jinni, which is a very powerful spirit obliged to obey its owner. Other examples of items with talismanic virtues include the self-setting table, the cornucopia, the purse of Fortunatus, and the refilling food bag of Arabic, African, Greek, and other European folktales. ✦

A rather interesting difference between talismans and other magickal items is that the talisman can influence its owner from a distance—it doesn't need to be in the right place at the right time. For example, when a husband gives his wife something personal before going into battle and asks her to keep it safe (which, in turn, extends protection to him), that object assumes the powers of a talisman. Although talismans are more potent than either charms or amulets— at least in terms of how far their energy extends—their power gets used up rather rapidly as a consequence. As you remember, Aladdin only got three wishes.

Fetishes

The word *fetish* probably comes from Latin *facticius* (artificial), by way of Portuguese *feitico* and French *fétiche*. Basically, a fetish can be any object. The important point is that the person who carries it must either have a strong emotional connection to the object or regard it as representing a higher authority (like a nature spirit or the Divine).

The cross of the Christian Church is, by all definitions, a fetish. It represents a higher power (Jesus), and many people carry or wear small crosses as items of protection and blessing. The rosary falls under this heading as well, representing the Virgin Mary, to whom prayers are directed for assistance.

✦ **Wiccan Wonderings: What's the best way to activate fetishes?**
There are several good ways to activate the energy of single-use fetishes. You can carry them, burn them, bury them, or float them on moving water. Burning releases your wishes to the heavens in the smoke and disperses the energy. Burying helps the energy grow. Floating in water helps transport the energy where it's desired. ✦

Fetishes are a little hard to describe outside the context of charms and amulets because they're very similar, except for their representative power and emotional connection. For example, if you are working with a love charm, you would use a picture of yourself and your loved one. Since the photograph has the power to evoke an emotional response, the charm could be considered a fetish. Similarly, a Pagan police officer might use her badge as a fetish because it represents a power (albeit mundane) and because she has it with her constantly.

In modern magickal practice, fetishes are most often used for one-shot spells. In such a case, the Witch makes up a bunch of fetishes at the same time, all of which have the same purpose. If a Witch uses a bay leaf (to represent Apollo) bound into a natural yellow cloth (for creativity) and empowers those bundles with an incantation, then he can use one of the bundles any time he feels the need.

The Advantages of Using Handy Magickal Objects
Charms, amulets, talismans, and fetishes are remarkably flexible and provide a great deal of creative leeway. They allow you to:

- Choose personally meaningful base components that support your magickal goals.

- Design particular items for long-term, short-term, or one-time use.
- Pattern the magick so it can be activated or turned off as needed.
- Create portable items that have the same energy signatures for which spells and rituals are devised; you don't have to carry spell components or all your ritual tools when leaving home.
- Fashion effective magickal tools in a reasonably short period of time.

People have always been creative in making charms, amulets, talismans, and fetishes. If one component wasn't available, they found something else that suited the task. As long as the symbolism held meaning and worked, they didn't fuss over having to make the substitution. This adaptability provides the modern Witch and Wiccan with a great prototype for using anything and everything in handy magick.

✳ Wiccan Wonderings: What if you're traveling and don't have traditional equipment and tools?
In a hotel, look at what's available. Soap can be charged as an amulet to protect against negativity. Mints are ideal as a charm for sweet communications. And if you find matches, bless and carry them with you to banish any darkness in your life. On an airplane, a napkin can be used to create a written charm for pleasant travel, and if snack items contain garlic, they can be eaten as amulets for protection. ✦

Adapting Spells
There will be many times when you will want to adapt a spell to suit your specific needs. But where do you begin the process? While adapting a spell is far easier than creating one, it still requires some forethought. When examining a spell, look for continuity and comprehensiveness:

1. Does the spell really target the goal at hand through its words, actions, and components?
2. Does it do so on a multisensual level (hearing, sight, touch, taste, and smell)?
3. Does every part of the spell make sense and excite your higher sentiments?

If the answer to any of these questions is no, you should try to find a substitute.

To illustrate, many old love spells call for blood as a component. But modern awareness of disease makes using blood inappropriate. Alternatives, then, would be to utilize a red juice or crushed berries that also have loving magickal qualities. Strawberry or passion fruit juice would work well. In this manner, you can still use the basic spell process while relying on components that are safe and support your ethics.

✳ **Wiccan Wonderings: Why did so many ancient spells include animal parts while modern ones do not?**
The ancients honored the power in nature by using it literally rather than symbolically. Since then, Witches have come to realize that this approach is neither ethical nor earth-friendly. Spellcraft and witchery have adapted to new times and societal situations, their powers growing with added symbolism. ✦

Creating Spells from Scratch
What's the difference between adapting a spell and designing one from scratch? Quite a bit. With the latter you no longer have a construct from which to work. You must devise all the actions, symbols, timing, wording, and other components of the spell. Following these steps will help you to create spells that can be just as effective as the existing ones you learn from this book and from other sources of Witchcraft and Wicca:

1. Boil down the purpose of the spell to a word or short phrase.
2. Find the ingredients suited to that goal (by using correspondence lists and resource books).
3. Consider the best possible timing for the spell.
4. Decide if you want a verbal component (incantation). If so, write it in a manner that includes your components and goal.
5. Bless all the items you will be using as part of the spell (this rids them of any unwanted energies).
6. Consider any actions that might help support the magick and where best to place them in the spell process (for example, lighting a candle at the outset to illustrate your intention).
7. Focus your will and begin the spell, building energy.
8. Guide the energy as far as you can mentally, then release it and trust in the outcome.
9. Keep a journal of your successes and failures for future reference.

Of course, it's not always necessary to use every step of this process. There will be instances when you can't conduct a spell at "just the right time," or when you don't have perfectly suitable components. The key is to have things as close as possible to that ideal state so that the resulting energy is accurate.

What kind of results can you expect from your spell work? Well, it depends on your focus, your willpower, and how detailed you get with the spell. Bear in mind that just like a computer, spells do what we tell them to do. So if you perform a spell to find a perfect companion and end up with a wonderful dog, your magick certainly has manifested! It just did so within a broader scope than you really wanted because you left out some details. Spells, being designed with energy, will always take the easiest and most direct route to manifestation, and their outcomes can be interesting—to say the least!

Chapter 6

Types of Magick

YOU HAVE ALREADY LEARNED about the basic tenants of Witchcraft and some of the general methods and tools of spellcasting. Before you jump into using that knowledge to begin working with specific spells for particular purposes, let's first explore a few of the various types of Witchcraft commonly practiced. While this is by no means a comprehensive overview of all magickal traditions, it will give you an idea of the various ways in which Witches put their craft to use.

Elemental Magick: Earth, Air, Fire, and Water

You now know that the four quarters (north, east, south, and west) have elemental associations—earth, air, fire, and water—that are relied on to gather the Sacred Circle and used in spellcraft and rituals. This section expounds on these associations and discusses elemental magick in more detail.

The elements are the four primary substances encompassing creation (all physical matter). But there is also a spiritual component to the equation. Following the Wiccan saying "As above, so below," Witches believe that each earthly thing also has a presence and form of expression in the astral world. Consequently, each element (earth, air, fire, and water) has been given astrological, mineral, plant, mystical, and lunar correspondences, as well as specific magickal attributes and personalities.

Earth: The Solid Element

In the eyes of a Witch, earth is the home of humans and all other beings, as well as a storehouse for all kinds of spiritual lessons. The earth element resides in the northern quarter of creation (the top of the sacred wheel). The magickal energies embodied by the earth element include patience, foundation, and harmony. Earth is the element in which the soul puts down roots so it can reach safely toward the heavens. Other traditional applications for the earth element include magick aimed at slow and steady progress, fertility, financial security, and overall abundance.

A good deal of earth's magickal symbolism is illustrated in global myths and superstitions. Nearly every tribal culture regarded earth in a maternal aspect. For example, there are Native American stories that tell us about how the soul waits for rebirth in the earth's womb (under the soil). Similarly, there are dozens of myths including those of ancient Sumer and Guatemala that describe humankind as being shaped from soil. According to the ancient Greeks, the heavens were born into existence from the womb of Gaia, the mother who oversees all the earth's abundance.

Many farming traditions include giving offerings of bread or mead to the soil to ensure a good crop. It is from this custom and various Roman planting rituals that Witches come by land and seed blessings today. In fact, soil was used as a component in many old spells. People buried symbolic items to banish something or to encourage growth. For example, to remove sickness, one healing spell instructs a sick person to spit in the soil and then cover that spot and walk away without looking back. To speed recovery from illness, patients were encouraged to grow health-promoting plants in the soil from their footprint. And if you wished to ensure a lover's fidelity, you would be advised to gather a little soil from beneath your foot and place it in a white cloth bag (for protection). It was said that your lover would never stray after that!

Air: The Elusive Element

Air resides at the eastern quarter of creation. Spiritually and mundanely, air is the most elusive of the elements because it is invisible, intangible, and very moody. It can be gentle or fierce, damp or dry, and each of these moods has slightly different magickal connotations. For example, a damp wind combines the power of water and air to raise energy that motivates and nourishes. The air element is applicable to traditional spells and rituals such as transformation, magickal dreaming, contemplation, renewal, working with spirits (ghosts), communication, and movement.

The ancients believed that the wind is influenced and changed by the corner of creation in which it originates. This idea translated into magickal methods quite nicely. If a wind is blowing from the south, it can represent fire and is said to generate passion, warmth, or energy for spellcraft. Similarly, a wind moving from the west brings water energies; from the north, it brings earth energies; and from the east, it doubles the strength of the air element!

We see a fair amount of directional wind work in spellcraft. For example, always scatter components in a wind moving away from you to carry a message or to take away a problem. Magick for new projects is best worked with the "wind at your back," for good fortune. When trying to quell anger, opening a window to "air out" the negative energy has great symbolic value, and, of course, when a Witch needs a wind, he or she has but to whistle! This is an ability said to have been passed down through families of Witches for generations.

Fire: The Element of Clarity

Fire takes up the southern quarter of creation. Magically speaking, the fire element empowers spells and rituals focused on banishing negativity or fear, dramatic purification, purity, enlightenment, power, and keen vision (the ability to see in the darkness). Because of its warmth, fire represents our passions, emotions, kinship, and an in-gathering of people. It was around the fire that our earliest tribes gathered to cook, tell stories, and celebrate life.

✳ Wiccan Wonderings: What is a Witch's power element?

Each Witch has one element to which she most strongly responds, called a *power element*. By working with and tapping into that element, a Witch can energize herself and her magickal processes. Determine your power element by going to places where you can experience each element intimately and paying attention to your reactions. Once you determine which element energizes you, find ways to expose yourself to it more regularly, to refill your inner well. ◆

In spellcraft and ritual, fire is generally used in one of the following ways. As the best source of light, fire is set up in a special way (usually without chemical additives) so its energy supports the gathering. Moreover, items are released to the fire either to destroy a type of energy or to release energy into the smoke (which in turn carries the desire to the winds).

Water: The Element of Movement

Magickally, water resides in the western part of creation. The magickal energies embodied by water include wellness, gentle transformations, movement, tenacity, abundance, and nurturing. Also, because the moon affects the tides, water has a lot of the same correspondences as the lunar sphere in its full phase for spell and ritual work.

A very popular application for water in spells and rituals is for healing and protection from sickness. According to European custom, dew gathered at dawn banishes illness, making it a good base for curative potions. Likewise, bathing in the water from a sacred well, dipping your hands into the ocean's water three times (then pouring it behind you so the sickness is likewise "behind" you), or releasing a token that represents your sickness to the waves are old spells that easily work in today's setting.

Spirit: The Fifth Element?

Spirit (also known as ether) isn't an element per se, but it is often included in a list of magickal elements as the fifth point of the pentagram. It's even harder to define than air. Spirit is the binding link between the four quarters of creation and thus the source of magick. Spirit resides within and without, around, above, and below all things. While we can experience earth, air, fire, and water directly with our temporal senses, Spirit is elusive and depends on both the Witch's faith and spiritual senses to be experienced.

In spells and rituals, Spirit usually comes into play if the Witch or Wiccan chooses to call upon a divine figure to bless and energize her magick. Alternatively, it can come into the equation if several devic (fairy) entities are being invoked and need to be able to work together. Spirit provides the medium in which any and all elements exist equally well.

Kitchen Witchery: Eat, Drink, and Make Magick

Kitchen magick (also known as hearth magick) is among the simplest schools of witchery and easily applies to many spiritual paths. Kitchen Witches are similar to Hedge Witches in their methods and outlooks. Although the Kitchen Witch may work alone or in an eclectic group, a Kitchen Witch definitely adheres to the keep-it-simple outlook. If something is available and contains the right symbolism, it's fair game for kitchen magick.

Functionality, Finesse, and Frugality

These are the keywords that describe a Kitchen Witch's approach to magick. Functionality, finesse, and frugality work hand in hand. If something is not functional, why expend time, money, and effort on it? With finesse, the Kitchen Witch brings personal flair and vision into every spell or ritual she performs. With frugality, the Kitchen Witch keeps magick affordable, enjoying a positive spiritual path without breaking the family budget. Looking to functionality, the

Kitchen Witch considers every item in and around the house as having potential for magick.

Ingredients for Successful Kitchen Witchery
The basic components for successful kitchen magick are:

Simplicity: This allows the Kitchen Witch to focus on the goal rather than the process.
Creativity: This allows the Witch to see the spiritual potential in even the most mundane items.
Personalization: This makes the practice meaningful, and it is the meaning that provides the most support for manifestation of the magick.

With this formula in mind, today's Kitchen Witches do not ascribe to the media's message that fancier is better. On the contrary, instinctive, intuitive things should come naturally, without a lot of fanfare. Kitchen Witches make every effort to keep Witchcraft part of their everyday life. Furthermore, kitchen magick should always reflect the individual Witch's principles. If you don't abide by these principles, you are not really practicing kitchen magick.

The Kitchen Witch's philosophy and focus begin and end at home. Wherever you live can function as your sacred space; what makes it "sacred" is how you treat it. Every item and action in the Kitchen Witch's life, from brewing coffee to brushing teeth, can be spiritual if she chooses it to be so.

The Folklore of Hearth Magick
Many Kitchen Witches look to folklore, superstitions, and old wives' tales for magickal ideas. A lot of magick resides in these old stories, and they are very easy to follow. For example, how often have you seen people toss spilled salt over their shoulder without a second thought? That practice comes from a superstition that tossing spilled

salt over your shoulder keeps evil away, and it gives the Kitchen Witch food for thought: Why not use salt (a common table condiment) as part of her magick for protection?

Kitchen Magick in the Kitchen

Of course, the ultimate expression of kitchen magick begins in the kitchen. Here you can make foods, beverages, potions, and notions that fill and fulfill body, mind, and spirit. To accomplish this, first do a little practical decorating. Hunt up some aromatic potholders, Witch-craft-themed trivets and refrigerator magnets, a candle or two, maybe even God and Goddess salt and pepper shakers!

✦ **Wiccan Wonderings: What is a Witch's personality element?**
Besides a power element, each Witch has a personality element. Earth people are grounded, like stability, plan everything, and have little patience for procrastination or flights of fancy. Air people are gypsy spirits who hate to be restricted and enjoy adventure, long conversations, and risks. Fire people are passionate and energetic (sometimes to the point of burning out); they dislike wishy-washy types with no spine. Water people like to go with the flow; they are healers, motherly types, and nurturers with unnerving psychic insights. ✦

Once the kitchen has a magickal feel, choose the tools for the job at hand: You can use a wooden spoon as a wand and a butter knife for an athame. These items are in your kitchen all the time, so they absorb your personal energy, and they maintain a congruity of symbolic value in your sacred space. You can use nearly anything that's handy and that has the right symbolism. Use straining spoons to strain out negativity, a blender to whip up energy, a microwave to speed manifestation, and dish soap for cleansing or asperging.

Steps for Making Magick in the Kitchen
1. Set up the space so it reflects your magickal needs and goals.
2. Choose kitchen tools appropriate to the working.

3. Choose your ingredients to support the process; in other words, match the magickal meaning of the foods, spices, and beverages with your goals and intentions. Don't forget to consider color and numeric symbolism as well. (This is also a good time to invoke the magick Circle.)

4. Chant, incant, visualize, sing. Empower whatever you're creating while you're making it. Make sure you do this at the most propitious time. For example, chant over bread while it's rising so the energy may likewise rise.

5. Serve the food in a manner that represents the desired manifestation. If you're working for joy, pattern the blessed food on the plate so it looks like a smile.

6. Say a prayer before using or consuming the results.

7. Trust in the magick.

It doesn't matter whether you're creating edibles, beverages, or just mixing up spell components that come out of the sacred space of home. What matters is that the meaningfulness is there, and the symbolism works in your mind and heart.

Food for the Spirit

People all around the world make spiritually enriched foods. For example, the Japanese eat a special glutinous-rice dish on their birthdays for luck, much as Americans eat cake. As recently as a century ago, folks still baked and brewed by the phases of the moon to improve the outcome of the recipe. Kitchen Witches revel in and embrace this approach to food magick.

For example, say you're preparing food for Samhain (Halloween), a festival for the dead. You might begin with potato soup (potatoes have eyes with which to recognize the spiritual world, and they help keep us rooted in this realm). Next, try a bean side dish for protection and insight. Black-eyed peas would work especially well here. For more safety, season the beans with onion and garlic. And for dessert, why not an apple or pumpkin pie to reflect the harvest? If making apple pie, make sure to rub the apples first (to rub away any "evil"); for pumpkin pie, carve the pumpkin first to chase away malicious spirits!

Magickal Properties of Common Culinary Items

Many of the edibles and spices in your home have various magickal associations. Here is a brief alphabetized listing of some of the items in your kitchen and their correspondences:

Alfalfa sprouts: frugality, providence
Anise: love, enthusiasm
Bacon: financial prosperity
Banana: male fertility
Bay leaves: energy, health
Beef: grounding, abundance
Bread: kinship, sustenance
Carrot: vision, the God aspect
Celery: foundations, peace
Chicken: health, new beginnings
Coffee: conscious mind, alertness
Eggs: fertility, hope
Honey: creativity, joy, well-being
Lemon: cleansing, longevity, devotion
Mint: rejuvenation, money
Olive: peace, spirituality
Pineapple: hospitality, protection
Potato: healing, foundations, earth energy
Rice: blessings, fertility, weather magick (rain)
Thyme: fairy folk, health, romance
Vinegar: purification
Wine: celebration, happiness

✦ **Wiccan Wonderings: How can a Kitchen Witch's magick be extended to other areas of the home?**

One simple way is to incorporate elemental decorating schemes, for example, place a shell in the west part of a room, a candle in the south part, a fan in the east part, and a potted plant in the north. Each item set up as an elemental point should be blessed and energized before it goes in place. Periodically, these items should be cleansed and re-energized, so they radiate only positive energy. ✦

Making House Candles

House candles are an important part of the Kitchen Witch's household repertoire. They honor the whole living space and represent the spirit of the entire house, including all past influences. The easiest approach is to make candles in fire-safe glass containers, which can be left burning for several hours at a time.

Melt the wax over a low flame. If you wish, you can add aromatic oils or very finely powdered herbs. This is also a good time to incant, chant, or pray, indicating your intentions in verbal form.

Put the wick into the glass container, keeping it in place by tying it to a pencil that is placed horizontally over the top of the container and adding a small weight (like a crystal) to make sure that the wick hangs straight down at the bottom. Let the wax cool slightly; then pour it slowly into the container. Cool and use as desired. Just make sure that the spell for which the candle is used somehow supports the goal of household harmony and peace!

Once you have a house candle, all residents of the house should be present the first time you light it. Each person's energy should be incorporated, so the candle itself becomes a representative of unity, trust, and love.

Green Witchcraft

Among the major talents cunning folk of old were noted for was a knowledge of herbs and how to use them. Wise country folk would carefully gather herbs at a certain time and prepare them with tenacity.

Be it in a potion or poultice, herbs and other plants were used for nearly every daily need—from healing and fertility, to giving star-crossed lovers a nudge.

Throughout history, various herbal remedies thought to have magickal properties eventually became what is known today as Green Witchcraft. The heart and soul of green magick is an intimate connection to, and appreciation of, nature. Green Witches consider every flower, leaf, blade of grass—yes, even weeds—alive and sacred, filled with magickal potential. Although it is somewhat connected with Wild Magick (the magickal properties of the animal kingdom discussed later in this chapter), Green Witchcraft is more focused on plants, flowers, trees, and herbs as a mainstay for components, symbols, and energy.

The tenets of Green Witchcraft are as numerous as the plants found on this planet. Some plants are recommended as helpmates to magick, while other plants seem to deter witchery. For example, rowan bound with red thread is one of the most popular antimagick charms. Or, to find immunity from the Witch's spells, carry marjoram flowers in your pocket. Plants that assist Witches include anise, which helps avoid the ire of an invoked spirit; eyebright or mugwort, which improves psychic awareness; or periwinkle, which increases the power of a Witch's magick.

Putting Belief into Practice

The first step in practicing green magick is to reconnect with nature. You can't honor something with which you have no intimate connection. The Green Witch strives to work in partnership with her plants. To that end, the Green Witch's garden is organic, and her household is one of diligent recycling. Living this way expresses the Green Witch's reverence for nature's gifts and ethical considerations in a practical way that brings the Green Witchery into daily life.

A Green Witch bring her philosophies and ideals into daily life and spiritual pursuits in lots of ways, including gathering loosened leaves and petals for magickal components (or to use in potpourri) rather than harvesting them; using plant matter as charms, amulets, and talismans; and adding plant matter to incense.

Natural Elements and the Sacred Space

To include plants in your sacred space, simply consider the symbolic value of the plant and its elemental correspondence. A variety of plants may serve as markers for the four elemental quarters of the sacred space. By choosing an item with the appropriate elemental association and putting it in the appropriate quarter, you honor the watchtowers and support the energy of the sacred space. When using a living plant isn't possible, it is perfectly acceptable to use a decorative item or an aromatic made from the appropriate plant. The following list contains some common plants and their elemental associations:

Earth (north): Alfalfa sprouts, beets, corn, fern, honeysuckle, magnolia, peas, potatoes, turnips, vervain.

Air (east): Anise, clover, dandelions, goldenrod, lavender, lily of the valley, marjoram, mint, parsley, pine.

Fire (south): Basil, bay, cactus, carrots, chrysanthemum, dill, garlic, holly, juniper, marigold, onions, rosemary.

Water (west): Aster, blackberries, catnip, cucumbers, daffodils, gardenias, geranium, iris, lettuce, roses, willow.

A plant's elemental association should also come into play with the time of the year. In the spring, air-oriented plants might decorate the altar, followed by fire plants in the summer, water plants in the fall, and earth plants in the winter. Of course, this correspondence may change according to their magickal tradition and is sometimes dictated by location and weather patterns, so this is only a generalized example.

Plants can also be used in the sacred space to honor particular Gods and Goddesses. Plants suited to whichever divinity the Witch plans to invoke into the space are placed on the altar or around the Circle. If, for instance, a Witch is working with Hera, a bowl of apples and a vase of irises would be suitable.

The remaining applications come in the enacting of the ritual itself. A Witch might use plants for asperging the sacred space (a branch of heather or woodruff are two favorites), wear them as head-pieces (wreaths of flowers and vines), or incorporate plants into her spellcraft. The limits are set by the goals of magick and the Green Witch's eye for creativity.

Sprouting Spells

At one time or another, nearly every plant on this planet has been used as part of a magickal spell. After all, the magick of plants and nature was always open to anyone who knew how to harvest its riches. All the traditional approaches to creating spells apply here (see Chapter 5), with the main difference being that the spell focus or key components are, of course, plants.

Exactly how the plant participates in the magick depends a lot on its symbolic value, the goal of the magick, and the spell construct the Witch devises. Typically, plants may be bundled, burned, buried, carried, floated, grown, or tossed to the winds as part of a spell.

- Bundling is typical of portable magick.
- Burning is a way of releasing a prayer or wish and sometimes is also used for banishing.
- Burying is used a lot in health-oriented spells.
- Carrying a plant is typically a type of charm or amulet.
- Floating can take energy away from or toward the Witch, depending on the water's direction.
- Growing supports progress and manifestation.
- Releasing plant matter to the winds carries the magick outward from the Witch.

Daisy, a very common flower, could serve as a working example. The daisy often appears in spells for love or to encourage fair weather. To incorporate daisies into your own magick, you could bundle three flowers and carry them as a love charm. You could also burn dry daisy petals in incense for fair skies, or release them to wind or water to take your wishes for good companionship to the four quarters of creation.

Or take pine as another illustration. Because of the heartiness of this tree, pine represents longevity, fertility, protection from evil, and peace. Witches also say that its aroma brings joy and prosperity. Carry pine cones with you to improve your outlook, or bury them around the home to safeguard it. Pine needles are excellent additions to dream pillows, helping to bring a peaceful night's rest.

Although these examples are limited, they provide a good foundation on which any Green Witch can build a spell repertoire using her favorite plants. Just one note: If you cannot grow your own plants, please make every effort to ensure that your components are organic—or at least very well washed. Chemical additives impede or dramatically change the magickal energies of any natural item.

Creature Craft

Although the days of animal sacrifice are long over for most Witches, animals have not disappeared from rituals and spells altogether. Cat whiskers, for example, are still used in wishcraft (magick that's based in wishing customs). If your pet is a familiar, a tuft of fur taken from his or her grooming brush might be used in spells to improve the rapport between you. A found bird feather might be used on the altar to represent the air element or to disperse incense around the sacred space.

Beyond these kinds of applications, small statues or images of animals sometimes become markers for sacred space, depending on the creature's elemental association. For example, a fish image might be placed in the west to represent the energies of water, whereas a lizard might be placed in the south for "fire" energies.

Additionally, some Witches carry the image of a creature as part of spells or charms with specific goals in mind. For instance, carrying a lion carving might be part of a spell for courage. If the carving is made from bloodstone, carnelian, or tiger's eye, all the better, because these stones have strong metaphysical associations with bravery.

Although using animal parts as offerings and spell components is no longer practiced, the power in each living creature (or its representation) has not been lost to modern Witchcraft. Other magickal uses of animals might include placing an image of an animal in the sacred space to represent the energy of a particular element, or enacting spells that protect beloved pets.

Animals as Messengers of Nature

Witches believe that the patterns and messages of the Divine exist in nature. The natural world is a wealth of knowledge that humans would do well to learn and integrate into their lives. Part of it is the knowledge of animals and their role in nature that Witches have relied on in their magick. There is a long-standing global tradition of animal magick that the modern Witch can tap into. ✦

Familiar Friends and Spiritual Signposts

Many Witches choose to have a familiar—a spiritually attuned creature to whom the Witch turns for insights into nature's lessons, and for help in magick. Today's familiars include cats, dogs, birds, bunnies, and even the stereotypical frog, but, really, any living creature with whom the Witch can have an ongoing relationship or rapport can fulfill the role of the familiar! Actually, the Witch doesn't necessarily choose this creature so much as the animal and the Witch seem to discover and bond with each other. No matter what kind of creature it might be, the familiar is no mere pet. The animal in question is the revealer of truths and a respected partner in every sense except being human!

If a Witch wishes to put out a call for a familiar, he usually does so through a spell or ritual. This ritual typically takes place outdoors, near the home. The Witch begins by creating sacred space, and then he meditates, prays, and places the request in the hands of nature. During the meditation the Witch visualizes the living space so the right creature can easily find its way to the door.

Power Animals and Totems

Power animals and totems also serve as helpers to Witches (as well as shamans). A power animal is a creature whose attributes you may take on for a short time, while that energy is "in play." For example, when you need to protect a beloved project, a she-bear guide may come into your life. These animals have strong associations with protective maternal instincts. By comparison, a totem animal seems more strongly attached to a person's spirit and often becomes a life-long spiritual companion.

Similar to finding a familiar, the process of discerning a power animal or totem often takes place in a ritualistic setting. Or, the animal spirit might reveal itself in a stray encounter, a dream, through repeated sightings in a variety of media, and so on. The key to success in this process is for the Witch to remain open to nature's voice and to avoid anticipating what her animal might be. While it would be wonderful to have a beautiful, graceful, powerful creature as a guide, that simply isn't always the case. Imagine the wonder of a Witch who discovered a bumblebee totem! It wasn't exactly an exciting discovery, but the symbolism made sense for her hard-working buzzing personality.

What happens when you discover your totem or power animal? The value of these energies varies a lot from culture to culture. What's important to remember is that an animal's symbolism embodies the whole creature: both its positive and negative aspects. The otter, for example, is playful, but it can also get very nippy. A Witch with an otter totem, therefore, needs to be aware that her biting sense of humor might take frolicking a bit too far.

Wild Magick

Familiars, totems, and power animals are part of Wild Magick, which covers a lot of territory. Wild Witches may include those from the fairy faith, shamans, earth healers, Green Witches, and proverbial tree-huggers. The main reason for such a broad diversity is the definition of Wild Magick. Essentially, the Wild Witch seeks to defend nature, deepen her understanding of the wild, use this understanding as a spiritual tool, and then educate others regarding the state of the earth and how to preserve it. That's a pretty big job, but one that many Witches, Wiccans, and Neo-Pagans embrace.

Wild Magick deals specifically with those moments when the "wild" world touches our nine-to-five reality in intimate ways. Animals represent a big part of that picture, especially the Witch's pets and familiars. Try the following strategy, a type of "wild" divination that relies on reading signs. Observe your pet's behavior with visitors in your home. It might give you some insights about your visitors you wouldn't otherwise get on your own, perhaps because animal reactions are based on instinct.

Outside the home, Wild Magick transforms a bit, especially when you're in a natural environment. For example, if a Witch observes gulls circling above a group of fisherman with their daily catch, he might gather up a stray feather and add it to his power pouch, in order to inspire extended vision, especially when hunting (figuratively). This, too, is Wild Magick: taking a gift from nature and applying it positively to your spiritual life.

Incorporating Animal Elements into Magick

Anyone who's read Shakespeare is familiar with the idea of using animal parts in magick: "Eye of newt and toe of frog, / Wool of bat and tongue of dog . . ." (*Macbeth*, Act IV, sc. 1). Where did this tradition come from? Quite simply, humans have always trusted animal spirits (and the spirits of plants and inanimate objects) for their powers. A magus who needed courage looked to nature's blueprint and found a lion, whose heart may be carried or otherwise used in a spell (thus the phrase "heart of a lion"). When a Witch needed stealth, it made sense to use the chameleon's skin as a spell component. When he needed perspective, a variety of birds came to mind, and he might harvest the eye.

Over time things changed, however. Only animal parts found in nature and properly cleaned are fit to be used magickally in Witchcraft. Modern Witches honor nature and her needs in their methods; eco-consciousness is a top priority.

Here's a brief list of animal components and applications you would likely find on a random walk in nature:

Antlers: Sliced antler makes a very sturdy carving surface, and may be used in making a personal set of runes. Alternatively, antlers can be carried to honor Artemis, Cernunnos, and Bacchus, or used as virility charms.

Eggshells: Traditionally, shells were buried or burned in healing spells (often after having been carried by the patient so the eggshells "absorbed" the illness). Eggshells also make a good womb symbol in which energy can be nurtured to maturity. Be sure to consider the color of the eggshell in the final application. For instance, use blue eggshells to nurture peace and joy.

Feathers: Use feathers for divination, for moving incense around the sacred space, or as a spell component in magick directed toward liberation and release. They're also good for meditations in which you wish to connect with bird spirits or the air element.

Fur: Tufts of fur can often be found on burrs or other prickly bushes. If you can determine the animal that lost the fur, you can apply the fur as a symbol of that creature and its attributes in spells and rituals. For example, a bit of rabbit fur would be a good component to put in your power pouch for abundance and fertility. (Any small pouch will do as a power pouch. Use it to keep special items, like small stones given by friends and those that carry personal meaning.)

Nails: Nails serve utilitarian purposes (for gathering food) as well as defensive ones—when in the clutches of a foe. With this in mind, animal nails could be carried as amulets and talismans for providence and safety.

Teeth: One of the longest-lasting parts of any body, teeth have natural associations with longevity and durability. Furthermore, teeth affect the way a lot of creatures communicate, so use them in different communication spells, depending on the type of creature involved. For example, if you were going into a meeting where clever discourse was needed, carrying a fox tooth might be apt.

Whiskers: According to an old bit of folklore, cat's whiskers that you find somewhere can be used in a wish-fulfilling spell. For this to work, burn the whisker and whisper a wish to the smoke. This spell might be accomplished with the whiskers of other animals too, like using a dog's whiskers to inspire devotion and constancy.

The Elemental Animal

Witches draw on animal symbolism to mark the sacred space. Specifically, they use animal images to denote the element of a quarter, to honor a God or Goddess, or to illustrate the theme of a working.

As with everything else on this planet, animals have particular elemental associations. These associations come out of the creature's environment and predominant behaviors. It's easy to see that fish are aligned with the water element, and therefore the western quarter. On the other hand, some animals have two common associations: A poisonous snake like an asp relates to both the earth and the fire element, because it dwells close to the soil but is also native to a sandy, hot environment and has a lethal bite.

Within the sacred space, any of the animals aligned with the energies of a specific quarter can watch over that quarter as an appropriate
representative. The following list provides the animals that embody
characteristics of the four elements, as well as their combinations.

Earth (north): Bear, cow, deer, ferret, gopher, mole, mouse,
   rabbit, snake
Air (east): Bat, most birds, butterfly, dragonfly, ladybug
Fire (south): Desert creatures, lion, lizard, scorpion
Water (west): Crab, duck, fish, seahorse, seal, whale
Water/air: Dolphin, flying fish, seagull
Water/fire: Electric eel
Fire/air: Bee, wasp, other stinging insects
Earth/water: Amphibians, beaver

Animal Imagery in Magick

Animal imagery may be used as a way of accenting a magickal working. Rituals
for earth healing, for endangered species, for a sick pet, to connect with the
Wild Magick within, and so forth, would all benefit from this type of visual cue.
The key is to choose the right animals for the goal of the ritual or spell. For
example, when casting a spell for a sick pet, the images should mirror that pet
(use photographs or at least images of a similar breed). ✦

Part 2

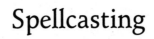

Spellcasting

Chapter 7

Spells for Love

SINCE THIS IS THE FIRST of many chapters on spells for specific purposes, a note on what you can expect from your spells is in order here. How quickly you get results from a spell depends, of course, on the clarity of your intent and your beliefs. If, in your heart of hearts, you really think this is all just mumbo-jumbo, then it's unlikely you'll see results. In that case, your time would be better spent working on changing that belief. On the other hand, if you're skeptical but open and receptive to the possibility that you live in a magickal universe and have the power to manifest what you need and desire, then you'll see results.

Sometimes when you do a spell, the situation seems to get worse before it gets better. This is possible with any kind of visualization exercise. Part of the reason is that when you consciously work with your beliefs and your intent, you're polarizing power within yourself, which helps rid you of negative beliefs. Once you're free of the negative beliefs, the situation improves.

The Truth about Casting Love Spells

Often, when we think of love spells, our minds conjure images of magickal incantations and mysterious potions meant to kindle the passions of a spellcrafter's otherwise indifferent object of affection. Fairy tales and Shakespeare aside, however, keep in mind that love spells aren't meant to enchant or bewitch someone into falling in love with you. We all have free will and nothing can violate that will—not even magick or spells. The true purpose of a love spell is to enhance and empower your own energy so you attract the individual who is the best for you.

Spells for love are numerous and varied, and before you do any, it's important to define what you want. Are you trying to attract someone? Looking for your soulmate? Hoping to enhance a relationship? The more specific you can be, the greater your chances of success.

Taking Emotional Inventory

Before you can fulfill your goals through spells, you first need to take inventory of your love life. The following questions apply whether you're single or committed and should give you a fairly clear idea about the patterns that run throughout your intimate relationships.

1. Describe your ideal intimate relationship.
2. Describe the worst intimate relationship you ever had.
3. How would you rate your present sex life?
4. If you're involved, is your significant other romantic?
5. Are you romantic?
6. If you're involved, is your relationship emotionally satisfying?
7. What, if anything, would you change about this relationship?
8. If you're not involved, jot down five important things you're seeking in an intimate relationship.
9. Describe the most satisfying relationship you have now. It doesn't have to be romantic; it can be with anyone—a child, a parent, a friend, or even a pet.
10. Do your love relationships have a spiritual component?
11. List five things you would like to change about yourself, then five things you love about yourself.
12. List five things you admire about the person you love most.
13. List five things that make you feel good.

Once you identify your patterns, it's easier to change them.

Loving Yourself

Loving yourself is a definite prerequisite for casting any love spell. It sounds simple enough, but so many of us have grown up believing that we aren't worthy, aren't attractive or intelligent enough, aren't this or that. Before you try any love spell, spend a little time uncovering your beliefs about yourself.

If you're holding on to negative beliefs about your worth as an individual, take a tip from author Louise Hay and adopt this simple yet powerful affirmation: "I love and approve of myself." Say it out loud, write it out, and post it on your mirrors, your fridge, and wherever else you will see it frequently. Yes, you probably will feel a bit foolish at first, but that just means the affirmation is working. When you repeat something often enough and back it with positive, uplifting emotion, your unconscious mind gets the message.

Putting Power Days and Astrology to Good Use

In astrology, the days of the week are governed by particular planets and the planets have specific meanings. In order to tip the odds in your favor, it's always good to align the type of spell you're doing to the most propitious day of the week. Since these are love spells, they should be done on Venus's night, Friday, unless stated otherwise.

The Days and Their Rulers		
Day	*Ruler*	*Meaning*
Sunday	Sun	Success, healing, happiness
Monday	Moon	Intuition, women, mother figure, creativity
Tuesday	Mars	Energy, passion, sexuality, aggression
Wednesday	Mercury	Communication, messages, the mind, the intellect, siblings
Thursday	Jupiter	Expansion, luck, success, higher education, the law
Friday	Venus	Love, art, beauty, money, women
Saturday	Saturn	Responsibility, structure, details

Another way to tip the scales in your favor when doing love spells is to use something that represents the other person's sun sign and element. If, for example, that person is a Taurus, you might want to enhance the earth element in your spell. Since water represents emotions and intuition, you could play up the water element, too.

Signs and Elements		
Signs	*Dates*	*Element*
Aries	March 21-April 19	Fire
Taurus	April 20-May 20	Earth
Gemini	May 21-June 21	Air
Cancer	June 22-July 22	Water
Leo	July 23-August 22	Fire
Virgo	August 23-September 22	Earth
Libra	September 23-October 22	Air
Scorpio	October 23-November 21	Water
Sagittarius	November 22-December 21	Fire
Capricorn	December 22-January 19	Earth
Aquarius	January 20-February 18	Air
Pisces	February 19-March 20	Water

A Simple Spell for Finding Love

This first love spell requires only a handful of rose petals (preferably given to you by a friend or loved one so they're already filled with good energy). Take them outside your house or apartment and scatter them on the walkway leading to your home, saying:

Love find your way,
Love come to stay!

Continue repeating the incantation until you reach your door. Retain one rose petal to carry with you as a love charm so love will follow you home.

A Spell to Attract a Lover

Tools:
1 pink candle
Ylang-ylang oil
Sandalwood oil
Lavender or your favorite oil
List of qualities
Pink pen
When: Friday, preferably around the New Moon, definitely during a Waxing Moon

This spell requires some forethought, because you'll have to come up with a list of qualities you're looking for in a lover. Do you have certain physical characteristics or personality attributes in mind? Write your list in pink ink; be specific, but brief.

Then, on or around the New Moon—or, at the very least, on a Friday night during the Waxing Moon, light your pink candle. Place your list next to the candle. Mix several drops of sandalwood oil, lavender oil (or your favorite oil) in your burner and light the candle inside of it. If the burner's candle is also pink, so much the better!

As the scent of the oil is released, imagine your lover. How does he or she look, act, and dress? What kind of car does this person drive? What type of work does he or she do? What are his or her passions? At the bottom of the list, draw the symbol for Venus: ♀

Continue the visualization for as long as you need to make the mental images as vivid as possible. Inhale the scent of oils from the burner. Snuff out the candle's flames rather than blowing them out. At least twice between the time you perform the spell and the next Full Moon, mix your oils and light the pink candle and the candle in the burner. As the scent permeates the air you breathe, feel the presence of your lover. As always, express thanks.

On the Full Moon, release your wish by throwing away both candles.

A Spell to Boost Your Confidence

Tools:
Ylang-ylang oil
When: Whenever you need a spiritual or emotional boost

Set aside a few minutes where you won't be interrupted. Dab a couple of drops of the seductive ylang-ylang oil behind your ears and on the inside of your arms. Vividly imagine what is going to happen when you're with the person you're going to see. Hold the images in your mind as long as possible, maintaining the vividness and detail. Then release the images with the certainty that everything will come to pass as you have imagined.

A Spell to Find Your Soulmate

Tools:
1 fresh rose
Rosewood oil
Ylang-ylang oil
1 pink candle
1 red candle
Empty glass container
When: On the New Moon, preferably on a Friday

The red rose, which symbolizes the love you're looking for, should be placed in a vase of water on your altar. Put several drops of rosewood and ylang-ylang oil in your burner. Place the candles in a shallow ceramic or glass bowl. Light your oil burner. As you light the candles, say:

Winds of love, come to me,
Bring my soulmate, I decree.
This I wish, so mote it be.

Imagine yourself with your soulmate. Be as detailed and vivid as possible in your imagining. Pour emotion into this visualization. Feel the potentiality of attracting this person forming in the air around you. Let the candles burn all the way down, so the pink and red wax flows together in the shallow bowl. While the wax is still warm, shape it with your fingers so the pink and red are fully blended. Run cold water into the bowl so the wax doesn't stick, then remove the newly shaped pink and red wax, and place it near the door of your home.

On the night of the Full Moon, release the wax by tossing it out; also toss out the now dried rose.

✦ Wiccan Wonderings: Is there a magickal tool that's good for attracting love?
Love incense will empower you and help to attract the person you desire. All you need is lavender, marigold, and rosemary. Charge the herbs under the light of the moon before you grind them (several hours of exposure should be enough). Then sprinkle them over incense coal, which is available at most New Age bookstores. When you know you're going to be around the object of your affection, just light the incense beforehand. ✦

A Tarot Love Spell

Tools:
Deck of tarot cards
Orange or lemon oil
Pink, red, or orange candle
When: Waxing Moon, preferably on a Friday when you're with the one you love

This spell is designed to draw the one you love closer to you. Choose whichever oil you like best (either one will do the job), and pick your candle color according to what you're trying to accomplish. Pink represents love, red represents passion, and orange represents balance.

During the Waxing Moon, before you're going to be with the one you love, put several drops of the oil you selected into your burner. Dip two fingers into the oil and anoint the candle with oil. Remove the suit of cups from your deck of tarot cards—it represents affairs of the heart. Then, select the king, queen, and 9 of cups (the wish card). Place the three cards on your altar, between the candle and the burner.

Light the burner and your candle, and state your wish. Be specific. Imagine it happening. Blow the candles out when you're finished, anoint them again with the oil, and place them in the area where you and your lover will be spending time together. When the two of you are in that room, make sure these candles are burning.

On the night of the Full Moon, light the candles again, state your wish once more, then snuff out the flames rather than blowing them out. Throw out the candles when you're finished and give thanks.

Variations on Tarot Spells

One variation of the tarot love spell is to select significators that represent you and the person you love. This method pegs the suits of the court cards to the elements. If you're a Gemini, for instance, and the one you love is a Sagittarius, then you would select a king or queen of swords to symbolize yourself and a king or queen of rods to represent the other person.

If you're doing a love spell that involves younger people, you would use the pages of the appropriate suits. If you're doing a spell that involves a pet, use a knight of any suit that feels right to you. If you know your pet's sun sign, use the appropriate suit.

A Spell to Enhance Your Relationship

Tools:
1 red candle
1 pink candle
Sprig of rosemary

Sprig of sage
Object that represents the enhancement or expansion of the
    relationship
When: A Thursday night during the Waxing Moon

You're doing this spell on Thursday because it belongs to Jupiter, the planet that signifies expansion, success, and luck. Before you begin your spell, light a sprig of sage and smudge the room where you'll be working. (This simply means moving the burning sage around the room so that its smoke passes over the walls and windows, the doorway, and your altar, purifying and cleansing the air.)

With the sage still smoking, place the pink and red candles at opposite ends of your altar, with the object that represents the expansion in the middle. Next to the object, place a sprig of rosemary. Now light the candles and the rosemary. Inhale the mixture of scents, shut your eyes, and imagine your relationship expanding in the way you want. Be detailed and make your visualization vivid.

Give thanks, then let the candles burn all the way down and toss them out.

☀ Wiccan Wonderings: How do you determine with whom you're most compatible?

In theory, the best match is someone whose moon sign is in your sun sign or vice versa. This would give you an instinctive understanding of each other. Another good match occurs when there are connections between sun, moon, and rising signs. The most passionate relationships often occur when the sign of your Venus matches another person's sun or moon sign. ◆

A Spell for Personal Empowerment

This spell is particularly good when you're in a new relationship and are feeling somewhat uncertain or unsettled about where the relationship is headed. It's also good for any situation or time when you need to feel personally empowered.

Tools:
2 gold-colored candles
Oil or sprig of frankincense
Sprig of sage
Deck of tarot cards
Pen and paper
When: The Full Moon

If at all possible, do this spell where the light of the Full Moon spills across your working area. Begin by lighting a sprig of sage to smudge the area where you'll be working and to increase your mental clarity. Next, remove the kings and queens from each of the four suits in your tarot deck.

If you're doing this spell for personal empowerment, simply select a king or a queen that represents the element of your astrological sign. (See the chart for element correspondences.) If, for instance, you're an Aries, Leo, or Sagittarian female, then you would choose the queen of wands. If you're doing a spell that involves another person, then select a king or queen of the suit that represents the element of that person's astrological sign. If you don't know the person's sign, allow your intuition to guide you in your selection of a card.

On the sheet of paper, write out your intent. Keep it simple and specific. Place the paper on your altar, with the card or cards on top of it. Put one of the gold candles to the west, the other to the south. Light the candles and the frankincense. Shut your eyes and visualize what you desire. Then say:

Spirits of the west,
Clarify my love,
Spirits of the south,
Empower me.
So mote it be.

Give thanks, let the candles burn down, then toss them out the next day.

Tarot and the Elements

Suit	Element	Correspondence
Rods/wands	Fire	Action, initiative
Swords	Air	Communication, intellect
Cups	Water	Emotions, intuition
Pentacles	Earth	Security, stability

A Spell to Enhance Your Sex Life

Do you or your significant other work such crazy hours that you never have time for each other? Does your home always seem to be filled with other people? Are your schedules so frantic that you both constantly seem to be moving in opposite directions? If so, this spell might be just the ticket.

Tools:
Ylang-ylang oil
Jasmine oil
4 red candles
Sea salt
Your favorite music
When: Full Moon or on a Tuesday, which is ruled by Mars

A Full Moon on a Tuesday is best for this spell, although a Full Moon on any day of the week works. But don't worry if nature doesn't suit your schedule and you find you're in the mood some night when there isn't a Full Moon—you can still get good results! First, draw a bath and sprinkle sea salt into the water. Sea salt is an excellent psychic and spiritual cleanser. Soak as long as it takes to relax fully—not just your muscles, but down to your very cells.

When you're completely relaxed, dry off and put on loose and comfortable cotton clothing. If you have set up an altar, put several drops of both oils into an aromatherapy container. Light the candle beneath it. As soon as the fragrance begins to permeate the air, place a candle in each of the four directions, beginning in the north and moving clockwise. As you light each candle, say:

> *Goddesses of the north and south, the east and west,*
> *Bestow your blessings, your power best,*
> *On me and him (her) to make us one*
> *It will be done.*

When you're finished, put the candles, still lit, into the bedroom or wherever you and your significant other will be. Let them burn out on their own. Wipe out the oil container and add fresh drops of the ylang-ylang and jasmine oil. The candle under the container should be lit when you and your partner are together, so that the fragrance suffuses the room where you make love.

A Spell for Fidelity

Many spells dealing with fidelity and bringing home a wayward lover are manipulative in that they attempt to influence the other person. While these spells often work well, they can also backfire. This spell focuses on you rather than on the other individual.

Just be sure of your motives if you're thinking of casting a spell for fidelity. Do you suspect that your significant other is being unfaithful? If so, do you really want to remain with that person?

> *Tools:*
> 4 candles of the appropriate colors for the four cardinal points
> Object that represents your lover
> Object that represents you
> Extra emphasis on water element (west)
> *When:* The Full Moon

Before you cast your Circle, make sure you have the objects you've selected on your working surface. Use sea salt to cast your Circle. As you light each candle moving clockwise from the east, visualize the element of each direction. Make the visualization specific.

As you face east (air), for example, you might breathe deeply and evenly and imagine your intellect as lucid, crystalline, capable of making the necessary decisions. For south (fire), you might imagine you and your lover passionately embracing. When you have finished lighting the candles, stand facing the east and say:

Winds of the east,
Goddess of the feast,
Keep (name of person) with me
So mote it be.

As you face south, say:
Fires of passion
Keep (name) close to me
So mote it be.

As you face west, say:
Waters of our hearts
Never do part
So mote it be.

As you face north, say:
Goddess of the earth
Keep (your name and other person's)
Together for now and ever more.
So mote it be.

Break your Circle. Let the candles burn out naturally, then bury them together in your backyard.

The Magickal Properties of the Sun Signs

These magickal properties can come in handy when casting spells for attracting love in general or a particular person.

Aries: Ruled by Mars, the God of war, you're a cardinal fire sign whose color is red.

Taurus: Ruled by Venus, Goddess of love and romance, you're a fixed earth sign. Your color is pale blue. However, some astrologers question Venus's ruleship; they feel that Taurus is actually ruled by the earth. Consequently, shades of brown work with your sign, too.

Gemini: Ruled by Mercury, the messenger. As a mutable air sign, your colors are the pastels.

Cancer: Ruled by the moon, you're a cardinal water sign. Your color is the hue of the ocean or the pale luminosity of the moon.

Leo: Ruled by the sun, you're a fixed fire sign. Your color is yellow.

Virgo: Ruled by Mercury, you're a mutable earth sign. Your color lies in earth tones.

Libra: Ruled by Venus, you're a cardinal air sign. Pastels are your colors.

Scorpio: Ruled by Pluto, the God of the underworld, you're a fixed water sign. Your magickal colors are the deeper tones: navy blue, magenta, and olive green.

Sagittarius: Ruled by Jupiter, you're a mutable fire sign. Your magickal colors are hot and luminous: hot pink and burning yellow.

Capricorn: Ruled by Saturn, you're a cardinal earth sign. Your colors are earth tones.

Aquarius: Ruled by Uranus, you're a fixed air sign. Your colors fall in the pastels, like those of Gemini and Libra.

Pisces: Ruled by Neptune, God of the sea, you're a mutable water sign. Your colors fall in the vast spectrum of blues.

A Charm to Safeguard Love

This charm requires all three elements of traditional charms: verbal, written, and physical. To work the charm, you will need red or purple construction paper (red and purple are the colors of passion and romance), rose oil, a picture of you and your mate, scissors, and a red pen. Dab the paper with the rose oil saying:

Rose of love, this charm's begun,
That I and _____ [name of your partner]
will always be one!

Cut the paper in the shape of a heart. In the middle of the paper put a picture of yourself and your beloved, writing your names underneath, and keep it in a safe place to safeguard that relationship and keep love alive.

Relationship Rescue Pie

If you're lucky enough to have found the right person, you might not need all of these spells to attract a lover or keep him or her faithful. Still, even a really great relationship hits some slumps every once in a while. Whenever your relationship is in need of a pick-me-up, try whipping up an apple pie. Maybe this doesn't sound very spell-like, but remember, Kitchen Witchery can be extremely useful. Besides, apples represent health, cinnamon is a good love herb, vanilla also inspires love, and ginger improves overall energy. So bake away!

Here are the ingredients:

8 medium apples, peeled and sliced thin
½ teaspoon ginger
½ teaspoon cinnamon
½ teaspoon nutmeg (or to taste)
½ teaspoon vanilla
¼ cup flour

2 pie crust sticks, prepared and rolled out according to directions
    on the box for a 9-inch pie, or from scratch
2 tablespoons butter

Directions:

1. Preheat the oven to 425 degrees. Toss the apple slices with the spices, vanilla, and flour; then put them into the bottom of the pie crust. Dot the top of the apples evenly with bits of butter. Put the other half of the pie crust over the top of the pie, securing it at the edges while saying:

    Secured within, so my magick begins.
    Transform anger with love, and bless from above!

2. Gently draw a heart in the top of the pie using a fork so that energy bakes into the crust. Bake the pie in the preheated oven for about forty-five minutes, or until the crust is brown and apple juice is bubbling through the heart pattern.

Chapter 8

Spells for Health

A HEALTH SPELL IS no different than any other spell. Its effect is dependent on your intent, your passion and beliefs, and your ability to focus. If you're doing a spell for your own health, *you* are the one who makes things happen. If you're doing a spell for someone else's health, the effects depend on the other person's willingness to be healed.

Health spells involve many of the same components that other spells do—herbs and incantations, visualizations and affirmations, colors and sounds. They also involve prayer, meditation, and touch. None of these things, however, is a substitute for treatment by a qualified physician or homeopath.

Taking Inventory of Your Health

By taking inventory of your health, you'll have a clearer idea about which spells will work best for you. Spend some time thinking about the following questions:

1. Most of the time, is your energy high or low?
2. When was your last visit to a doctor? Why did you go?
3. Do you have regular checkups?
4. Do you have chronic health problems? If so, what are they?
5. Do you get several colds a year?
6. How much sleep do you need each night?

7. When do you feel happiest and healthiest?
8. Are there certain times of the year when your health is better or worse?
9. Do you worry a lot about your health?
10. Do you worry about death?
11. Do you experience fluctuations in your moods?
12. Do you consider yourself a basically optimistic person?
13. Do you have a particular spiritual belief system?
14. In general, how would you describe your health?
15. Have you noticed any particular patterns to your health?
16. Describe your beliefs about illness and health.
17. Have you ever sought alternative treatments for an illness or disease?
18. Do you meditate?
19. Does anyone in your family or close circle of friends have a chronic illness? If so, what type?
20. Do you consider yourself an open-minded individual?

Pay special attention to your answers for questions concerning your beliefs about health and illness. It may be that the three colds or the flu you get every year is directly related to your belief that getting three colds a year or coming down with the flu during the winter is normal. Read your answers several times. If you find that you hold negative or limiting beliefs concerning health, then changing these beliefs will do more for you than any spell.

The Human Energy Field

"Your body is designed to heal itself," writes Donna Eden in *Energy Medicine*.

In fact, we have all the tools we need to heal ourselves, and it begins with an awareness of the subtle energies that give our bodies life. In China, these energies are called *chi* or *qi*. In India and Tibet, the energy is known as *prana*. The Sufis call it *baraka*. It runs through meridians in our bodies and is contained in seven major centers, or chakras, that extend from the base of the spine to the crown of the head.

Chakra literally means a disk or vortex. Imagine a swirling center of energy of various colors and you'll have a pretty good idea of what it looks like. When our energy is balanced, we are healthy. When our energy centers are unbalanced or blocked, we get sick. Each energy center has a particular function and governs certain organs and physical systems within its domain. When a chakra is blocked, unbalanced, or not functioning properly, the organs and systems within its domain suffer the effects.

The energy centers are said to contain everything we have ever felt, thought, and experienced. They are our body's data banks in this life and are imprinted with our soul's history throughout many lives. Illness manifests first in the body's energy field, where it can be seen by an individual who can perceive the field.

When a medical intuitive, for instance, looks at an energy field, he or she is able to perceive a number of details. To a medical intuitive, your chakras make you an open book. You don't have to be a medical intuitive, however, to pick up information about your health or the health of someone else. Sometimes, simply going with your first intuitive impression, going "from the gut," is enough.

Emotional Patterns and the Energy Centers

As you work with your own energy centers through spells, your system will be unique to you. The more you learn about the human energy system, the better equipped you are to maintain your health.

The first energy center is what Carolyn Myss, Ph.D., author of *Sacred Contracts, Anatomy of the Spirit,* and many other books, calls "tribal power." It relates to our families, our framework in life, and where our basic needs are met as children. It's where we learn to trust and to help ourselves. When this center isn't working the way it should, we may experience chronic lower back pain, sciatica, rectal problems, depression, and immune-related disorders.

Myss calls the second center "power and relationships." The issues governed by this chakra have to do with individuating ourselves from our tribe—our family. Power issues are invariably involved over our autonomy, money, sex, blame and guilt, creativity. Money worries often manifest in this area. When this chakra doesn't function correctly, we may have trouble with our reproductive organs, bladder, urinary tract, hips, and pelvis.

The third energy center is what Myss calls "personal power." It is dominant when we're in puberty and are attempting to establish who we are, our "ego self." Issues involved are trust, responsibility for making our own decisions, and our self-esteem. Mona Lisa Schulz, M.D., intuitive, and author of *Awakening Intuition*, says this energy center is about "me against the world." When the center is off balance, we have problems such as ulcers, Crohn's disease, anorexia or bulimia, addictions, liver trouble, obesity, and adrenal dysfunction.

This center is where many of us experience intuitive insight. A "gut hunch," for example, originates here.

The lower three centers, says Myss, are where most people spend their energy. "Most illnesses result from a loss of energy from these three chakras." Both Myss and Schulz note that even when someone develops a disease related to the upper chakras—heart or neurological problems, for example—the energy origins of the illnesses often come from the bottom three chakras.

The fourth center is known as the heart chakra. It's all about our emotions—how we feel or block them, how we express them, and to whom we express them. It's about identifying what we feel at any given moment. Once we know what we feel, we can take steps to change what needs to be changed in our lives. When this chakra isn't functioning correctly, the physical problems that can result include asthma and allergies, lung cancer, heart attack, bronchial pneumonia, and breast cancer.

The fifth center, the throat chakra, has to do with personal will and expression. This is the area that's engaged in spell work. It also involves issues such as pursuing and living our dreams, timing, the way we express what we want, and our capacity to make decisions. "Health in this center," writes Schulz, "calls for a balance between expressing ourselves and listening to others; between pushing ourselves forward to fulfill our needs or waiting, when necessary, for things to come to us; and between imposing our will on others or allowing others to impose their will upon us."

Energy Centers and Health (Based on Carolyn Myss's System)

Chakra	Where	Organs and Systems
1	Base of spine	Immune system, rectum, feet, legs, bones
2	Below navel	Sexual organs, large intestines, appendix, hips, bladder
3	Solar plexus	Abdomen and stomach, upper intestines, liver, kidneys, gallbladder, pancreas, middle vertebrae, adrenal glands
4	Between nipples	Heart and lungs, shoulders and arms, circulatory system, diaphragm, ribs, breasts, thymus gland
5	Throat	Throat, neck, thyroid, parathyroid, trachea, esophagus, mouth, teeth, gums, hypothalamus
6	Middle of forehead	Eyes, ears, nose, brain, nervous system, pineal and pituitary glands
7	Crown	Skeletal system, skin and muscular system

When this chakra isn't functioning the way it should, we may experience problems with our throats, gums, and mouths. We may get swollen glands or have thyroid problems. Quite often, the smooth functioning of this chakra depends on expressing what's in our fourth center, in our hearts.

The sixth energy center concerns thought and perception. Its issues concern our intellectual abilities, openness to new ideas, our ability to learn from experience. When this chakra doesn't function correctly, the physical problems, such as brain tumors and stroke, or neurological problems such as Parkinson's, seizures, spinal difficulties, and problems with the ears, eyes, and nose, can creep up.

The seventh energy center concerns our spirituality and being able to integrate it into our daily lives. It involves finding a sense of our life's purpose. "The failure to connect with our purpose affects us profoundly in the seventh emotional center," Schultz says. In some instances, this failure can prove fatal. After all, if you don't have a reason to live, your body simply shuts down. This energy center is about taking responsibility for creating our own lives.

Some of the physical problems that can occur when this center doesn't function properly are chronic exhaustion, Lou Gehrig's disease, multiple sclerosis, and what Myss calls "energetic disorders."

This is by no means a complete list of emotional patterns related to the various chakras. But it should provide enough information to use the spells in this chapter.

✦ **Wiccan Wonderings: Can you see the human energy field?**
The human energy field extends from a few inches to several feet around the physical body. It's like our personal ozone layer, a buffer. When it's healthy, the colors are brilliant and smooth, but illness and disease may cause it to have dark or white splotches in it, tiny rips or tears or discoloration. With practice, anyone can train themselves to detect the aura. Some people may see it, others may feel it, and still others may do both.

A Spell to Bolster the First Chakra

> *Tools:*
> Object that represents your "tribe"
> 1 red candle
> Pen and paper
> *When:* Whenever you feel the need

Create a Strength and Safety Amulet

The idea for this amulet comes from India. To make the amulet, go out at dawn and pluck a small piece of bark from the east side of a tree (where it gets the morning light). Bind this with a piece of yellow or gold-toned yarn, saying:

> Gathered from where the sun awoke,
> The power of protection and strength I invoke!

Wrap the bark in a natural white cloth (so it won't get damaged) and carry it with you often.

For this spell, you're addressing first chakra needs—your "tribe," your ability to provide for life's necessities, your ability to stand up for yourself, and any of the organs and parts of the body that are governed by the first energy center.

The object that represents your support system can be anything—a family photo, a photo of coworkers, a figurine of an animal, something you bought on a trip. It doesn't matter, as long as it symbolizes your tribe.

Jot down what you're trying to accomplish. If you're mired in depression, write an affirmation. "I am happy" or "My mood is great." If you feel insecure within your tribe, then write "I am safe and secure" or some other variation of the idea that feels right to you.

Slip the paper under the symbol, light your red candle, and say your affirmation aloud. Visualize the end result. As always, back it with emotion. Then burn the paper; releasing your desire, let the candle burn down on its own, and toss it out.

You can also apply variations of this spell for each of the seven energy centers.

A Spell for a Specific Ailment

First, try to locate the ailment in terms of the energy centers. If the ailment isn't listed in this chapter, then use what you do know. If, for instance, you have a sinus infection, then you would focus on the sixth chakra, which governs, among other things, the nose.

Ask yourself questions in terms of the sixth chakra's themes. Are you closed to new ideas? Are you feeling inadequate? You might also want to look at the themes for the third and fourth chakra to see if these fit you.

Once you've decided which chakra or chakras to work with, write an affirmation that states what you want. For a sinus condition, your affirmation might be: "I am at peace." Or: "I am well." Light the appropriate colored candle for the chakra you're working on. Focus your full attention on that chakra and vividly imagine the energy in that area in a spinning clockwise motion.

Do the visualization as long as you can maintain the energy. Then say the affirmation aloud, burn the piece of paper on which you wrote it, blow out the candle, and toss it out.

A Spell to Get Rid of a Headache

If aspirin doesn't work, then maybe this will. Rinse a quartz crystal with salt water, then "charge" it in the sunlight for a while. Hold it to your forehead for several moments and imagine the quartz absorbing the pain. When you're finished, cleanse and charge the crystal again. This is a good method to use for another person's headache, too.

A Spell for Maintaining Health and Vitality

Take an old knitted glove that you've worn and stuff it with healthful dry herbs (symbolically, you are stuffing yourself with all that positive energy). Some good options include caraway, coriander, fern, geranium petals, juniper, marjoram, nutmeg, tansy, and thyme. When you're done, sew up the opening (so the health remains where you put it), tie a strand of your hair around the pointer-finger of the glove (to remind you of good health and its blessings), and keep this with your clothing.

Strength and Safety Soup

Here's a recipe to use during those times when you feel you need more protection. Garlic and onions are the key ingredients. Romans used garlic for strength, and many other people have considered it a protective herb. Egyptians used onions to keep away baleful spirits and fed them to their slaves to ensure vitality. This recipe also relies on the number four for its earthy energy, which provides the magick with foundations to take root in our hearts and lives.

Ingredients:
1 large Spanish onion
1 large red onion
1 bundle green onions
1 white onion
4 sticks celery, diced (optional)
1 tablespoon butter
4 small cloves garlic, peeled and crushed
2 cups beef stock
2 cups chicken stock
2 cups water
4 dashes (1 tablespoon) Worcestershire sauce (or to taste)
Garlic powder and onion power (optional)
Croutons and grated cheese (for garnish, optional)

Directions:
1. Slice the onions and place them in a frying pan with the butter and garlic.
2. For a heartier broth, add 4 sticks of diced celery (to be fried with the onions). Magickally, this ingredient will provide you with psychic insight and a sense of inner peace.

3. Gently sauté the onions and celery, if desired, until golden brown.
4. Stir the vegetables counterclockwise as they cook to banish negative energies, saying:

    Onions for health, and to keep ghosts at bay,
    Garlic for safety all through the day!

    Keep repeating the incantation slowly until the onions are done.
5. Transfer the onions into a large soup pan, adding the stock, water, and Worcestershire sauce (you might also add a bit of garlic powder and onion powder, but that's optional). Cook this mixture down over a medium-low flame until it is reduced by two cups.
6. Serve the soup with croutons and fresh grated cheese, if desired. Visualize your body being filled with white light as you eat it.

Casting a Health Spell for Another Person

Tools:
Something that represents the other person
Sprig of sage
Eucalyptus oil
1 gold candle
1 purple or violet candle
When: As needed

You can use a photograph of the person or an object the individual has lent or given you. Set it in the middle of your work area or altar, with a candle on either side of it, and the oil burner behind it.

Smudge your work area first and also smudge the object that represents the other person. Pour several drops of eucalyptus oil into your burner. Light it, then light the candles. After a moment of reflection in which you fix the person's face and being in your mind, say:

As the oil and candles burn,
Illness gone and health return,
For my (state relationship and name)
Who is yearning,
And so deserving.

Blow out the candle in the oil burner. Let the other two candles burn down naturally, then toss them out.

✳ **Wiccan Wonderings: What needs to be considered before casting a spell for another person's health?**
First, always ask that person's permission. It may be that the illness or disease the person has serves some function in his or her life. The individual may not see it this way, but on some level, it may be true. Even when you do get permission, stick to a general spell to bolster the individual's overall physical health rather than work on any specific area or complaint. ◆

A Spell to Boost Your Energy
Sometimes, we just feel *depleted*. We need a day off from work simply to laze around and read, go swimming, or take a long walk in the countryside. We aren't sick, we aren't recovering from any illness—we just need to refuel ourselves. For those times, this is the spell you need.

Tools:
Your favorite music
Rose quartz
Vervain
When: As needed

This spell is best done when you're alone because you're going to crank up the music. Select music that boosts your spirits and makes you want to move around and dance.

Essential Oils for Health

Essential oils can be helpful in the health area. Here are some common uses:

1. For warts, try one drop of lemon essential oil applied directly to the wart, daily until it disappears.
2. When you overindulge, try essential oils of juniper, cedarwood, lavender, carrot, fennel, rosemary, and lemon. Make your own blend of these oils and use a total of six to eight drops in a bath.
3. To relieve depression, make a blend of geranium, lavender, and bergamot in a room diffuser or put six to eight drops in a bath.
4. Rosemary promotes alertness and stimulates memory. Inhale during long car trips or while reading and studying.
5. For restful sleep, put one or two drops of chamomile, lavender, or neroli on your pillow before going to bed.
6. For burns or scalds, apply tea tree oil directly to the affected area.
7. To aid digestion and relieve an upset stomach, put one drop of peppermint oil in half a glass of water and sip slowly.
8. To relieve teething pain in children, use one drop of chamomile oil on a washcloth wrapped around an ice cube.
9. To cool the body in summer and protect it in winter, use one drop of chamomile oil in the bath.
10. When the flu is going around, add a few drops of thyme oil to a diffuser or let it simmer in a pan on the stove.

The rose quartz is intended to amplify the surge in your mood. The vervain, when burned, provides a general boost to the spirit and cleanses negative vibes, among other things.

Light the vervain, put the quartz next to it, then put on your music and turn the volume up. Let the music suffuse the room and permeate your senses. Then get up and dance to it. Continue as long as needed.

Chapter 9

Spells for Luck, Prosperity, and Abundance

ASK ANY OF YOUR FAMILY, friends, and acquaintances what prosperity and abundance mean to them, and the responses are sure to span a broad spectrum. Answers might range anywhere from having enough or more money, being rich, or being in a better job; to having a strong, loving marriage or significant relationship; to writing a bestselling novel. Whether it's owning a horse or owning a home, the answers are always different. Most people yearn for prosperity and abundance, yet these concepts are rather abstract.

What about your own personal view? Do you define prosperity in terms of financial security? Or is your idea of prosperity more about having good health and happiness? Does abundance mean having more of everything or having enough of everything? These distinctions may seem unimportant, but before you work with spells involving prosperity and abundance, it's wise to recognize what these concepts mean to you.

Defining Your Concept of Prosperity and Abundance

Our lives are in a constant state of flux. Once that horse is owned, that novel hits the bestseller lists, or that ideal relationship is found, our ideas about prosperity and abundance change accordingly. Think about what prosperity and abundance mean to you *today, right now, in this moment*. Finish the phrases below with your true feelings, but don't think too hard about them. The idea is to bypass your rational left brain and allow your intuitive right brain to express itself.

1. I am happiest when . . .
2. My wildest dream is to . . .
3. Given the choice, I would most like to spend my time . . .
4. I thoroughly enjoy . . .
5. I would love to . . .
6. I now spend my free time . . .
7. I feel a sense of accomplishment when . . .
8. My greatest passion is . . .
9. One of my favorite hobbies is . . .

In this exercise, you identified things that make you feel happy and prosperous. Now find an object that represents each entry on your list. Select these objects with care; they're going on your altar and will be used in spells.

Let's say that your wildest dream is to get your pilot's license. Any number of objects might be selected to represent that dream: a model airplane, a photograph of the type of plane you would like to fly, even a child's plastic toy plane. The point is to choose something that immediately connects you to the *feeling*.

Once you've selected your symbolic objects, you're ready to prepare your altar.

More about Altars

Earlier, we discussed your power spot. Your altar, if you choose to have one, goes in your power space. (If it's outside, you might have to create something more portable.) An altar is merely a special place you create that contains objects symbolizing who you are and what you desire. It doesn't need religious connotations or dogmas attached to it. In fact, if the word feels uncomfortable, then call it something else.

This place is *yours*. You can put whatever you want on it—fresh flowers, sticks of incense, candles, photographs, statues, figurines, a bowl of fresh water. . . . The objects you place on your altar should also include the ten objects you selected to represent the things and experiences that make you feel prosperous and abundant.

Be Careful What You Wish For

At some point in your spellcasting, something will drive home the truth of the old adage, "Be careful what you wish for. You may just get it." This adage speaks to the power of intent. If you ask for abundance or financial freedom, consider your wish carefully. How will that abundance or financial freedom affect your family? Your relationship with your friends? Your job and living situation? Unforeseen repercussions have a way of creeping up, so think things through! ◆

Candles are great objects to include on your altar. They represent illumination and also signal to your conscious mind that something is beginning. Lighting a stick of your favorite incense or putting out fresh flowers triggers your sense of smell. Water aids in the focus of your intuition. Also try to have each of the four cardinal points represented on your altar. The idea is to ritualize this time you are setting aside for yourself.

If you decide to set up your altar permanently in your power spot, then the consistency of the place sends a message to your deeper self that you mean business. The physical location can be virtually anywhere you want it to be. A garden will do as well as a corner of a room, as long as it's a spot where you won't be disturbed.

In Wicca, an altar is the heart of the Circle that's cast for doing spells. In this chapter, though, none of the spells requires that you cast a Circle. So at the beginning, keep your altar simple.

The Color of Money

In terms of spells, the color of money is green. In other words, if you don't have prosperity consciousness—the belief that you are deserving—then you need to develop it before you attempt a spell for prosperity.

Louise Hay, writing in *You Can Heal Your Life,* devotes a chapter to prosperity. She provides a list of negative money beliefs and then illustrates how you can change any of the beliefs you may hold. For prosperity, she writes, it's necessary to:

- Feel deserving
- Make room for the new
- Be happy for other people's prosperity
- Be grateful

To these, she adds, "Love your bills."

"What?" you're probably saying. "My credit card bills? My electric bill? My mortgage payment? *This woman's crazy.*" But the more you think about it, the less you'll balk. After all, a bill is simply an acknowledgment that a company trusts that you can and will pay—a sort of cosmic honor system. Why should you resent it? Money and prosperity are expressions of living in a universe that is infinitely abundant. All of us can tap into that abundance without depriving someone else. It simply boils down to belief.

While you're building your new belief in prosperity, make symbolic gestures, as mentioned earlier in this book. Drop your loose change into the Salvation Army pot at Christmas. Buy yourself something special. Treat yourself to dinner at your favorite restaurant. Buy a hardback book that you really want. Create your own affirmation about prosperity—and always phrase it in the present tense. Write or say it at least a dozen times a day for as long as it takes for your unconscious to get the message. *Be sure to back that affirmation with emotion.*

And post this quote from Louise Hay's book in a spot where you'll see it frequently: "True prosperity begins with feeling good about yourself . . . it is never an amount of money; it is a state of mind. Prosperity or lack of it is an outer expression of the ideas in your head."

A Spell to Create New Beliefs

Tools:
14 green scented candles
1 empty glass container
When: On the New Moon

While you're still in the process of writing your affirmation, buy fourteen scented green candles. Small candles are good for this, the kind that are sold for aromatherapy burners. On the night of the next New Moon, light one of the candles at your altar or special place. While it's burning, say your affirmation aloud and feel its truth. After five minutes, blow the candle out and rub your hands in the smoke. Wave the smoke toward your face, your body, your clothes. Remember that fragrance, associate it with abundance, prosperity, and your new belief. Set the candle aside where you can see it.

✦ **Wiccan Wonderings: What's the most important ingredient in any spell?**
It always boils down to belief. Remember, Dorothy got back to Kansas because she trusted the wizard when he told her all she had to do was close her eyes and click her heels three times. It worked because she believed in magick. ✦

Repeat this for the next fourteen days, using a new candle each time, until the next Full Moon. Set each spent candle next to its predecessor. On the night of the Full Moon, after you have burned the fourteenth candle, light all fourteen and let them burn down. Then pour the wax into a glass container.

This candle symbolizes your new belief about prosperity. Once the wax has solidified, toss it out, thus sending that belief out into the universe.

Each time you do this spell, remember to give thanks.

A Spell to Fulfill Your Desire

Tools:
1 green scented candle
An object that represents your desire (choose from your list)
When: During the Waxing Moon

At night, under the waxing phase of the moon, light a green candle at your special place. State your need or intention. Place or focus on something on your altar that represents this need or intention and repeat your affirmation. Visualize the manifestation of whatever it is you need. Don't worry about how it will manifest; simply trust that your wish will be fulfilled. Blow out the candle and leave it and your symbolic objects on the altar. Be grateful for all that you *do* have.

Repeat as often as you feel is necessary during the Waxing Moon. When you trust that what you need is forthcoming (and yes, this does take trust), clear your altar and let the candle burn all the way down. Then toss it out and release it.

A Spell to Increase Your Income

Tools:
Green and white candles
A deck of tarot cards
An object that represents your desire (consult your list again!)
A pen with green ink and a piece of paper
When: During the Waxing Moon

The color green is obviously important in money spells. White, however, can also be useful because it represents understanding.

Put your candles at opposite ends of your altar. Between them, place an object that represents your desire to increase your income.

This can be an object that symbolizes something on your list or anything else—a coin, a dollar bill, a sacred stone, whatever you want.

From your deck of tarot cards, remove the suit of pentacles or coins, which represents money, and the Star and the 9 of cups. In front of the white candle, place the ace of coins; it symbolizes new financial undertakings and opportunities. In front of the green candle, put the 10 of coins; it's called the "Wall Street" card and symbolizes a financial windfall. In the middle of the two candles, place the 9 of cups—the wish card—and the Star, which symbolizes, among other things, success.

Now light the candles and say:

The money I spend
or the money I lend
comes back to me
in multiples of three.

Visualize the figure you have in mind. Jot it down on the piece of paper. Imagine what you can do with an increase in your income. The more vivid you can make your visualization, backed with intense emotion, the faster it will manifest. This ritual can be as short or as long as you want. The point is to do it with full conscious awareness and intent, backed with emotion. End the spell by blowing out the candle and giving thanks, then toss away the candle.

On the next night, repeat the ritual, but with certain changes. First, remove the 2 and 5 of pentacles from your deck. You don't want these two cards on your altar. The 2 of coins means you're robbing Peter to pay Paul; the 5 means poverty and heavy debt.

Light your candles. Say the poem. Then take the remaining cards and place them between the ace and 10 of coins and the wish card and the Star. Visualize, affirm, then blow out the candles and throw them away. Keep everything else on the altar as it is overnight.

✦ **Wiccan Wonderings:** ~~What can you do when money seems to be~~ going out faster than it's coming in?

Here's a quick fix: Buy a roll of purple, violet, or lavender ribbon—the kind you find in the gift wrap area of most drug stores and supermarkets. Tie a piece of ribbon around every faucet in your home, and as you do so, say: "As water flows, my finances grow." ✦

On the third night, light the candles and give thanks for everything you have; repeat the poem and feel the reality of your increase in income taking form around you. Blow out the candles and toss them away.

Keep saying the poem as long as you need to, as often as you like, even after the increase begins to manifest.

A Spell to Say Goodbye to Debt

Tools:
1 red candle
Tarot's 5 of coins
Empty bowl
When: During the Waning Moon

Remember that even quick and easy spells must be done with vivid intent and visualization. In terms of tools for this one, you can substitute something for the 5 of coins that represents your debt, but make sure it will burn.

Light the red candle. Red represents energy and what you're doing here is drawing on energy to cancel your debt. Say the following words:

Debt begone
lickety split,
debt begone
before I spit.

Then take the five of pentacles or whatever object symbolizes your debt and pass it through the candle flames until it catches fire. Let it burn to ashes in the empty bowl. Pinch out the candle's flame, then toss out the candle. On the next New Moon, bury the ashes far from your home.

A Spell to Create Prosperity

Tools:
Sprig of sage
1 green candle
Empty bowl
Pinch of cinnamon
When: During the New Moon

This spell can be used for any kind of prosperity, but it works best for the prosperity of inner peace, the source of all true prosperity. Sage is a good herb for getting rid of negativity and cinnamon is excellent for boosting your energy and creativity.

On the night of the New Moon, put the green candle in the empty bowl with the sage. Light them both. As you sprinkle cinnamon into the flame, say: "I embrace prosperity and inner peace."

Repeat these words and keep sprinkling cinnamon into the flame until the cinnamon is gone. Let the candle and the sage burn down, then bury them in your garden or yard. If you do this during the winter, you can bury the remains in the dirt of an indoor plant.

An Oil to Attract Money

Tools:
1 pint mineral oil
A clear quart bottle
7 lodestones (found in most New Age bookstores)
A pinch or two of iron filings

This oil works for attracting things other than money, too. Pour the mineral oil into the bottle, add the lodestones and iron filings, then charge your concoction in the sunlight, preferably when the sun is rising, for seven days. Transfer your oil to smaller bottles with dark glass, label them, and put them in the dark. To bring in money, rub some oil on your thumb and forefinger, then rub your fingertips on money before you spend it. The idea is that the charged, magnetic oil will attract money into your life.

A Spell to Attract Financial Opportunities

Before you do this spell, read the section in Chapter 7 on the correspondences between astrological planets and days of the week. Also glance through Chapter 3 to refresh your memory about the importance of the cardinal points in casting spells.

Tools:
1 gold candle
Your favorite scented oil
Clear quartz crystal
Pen and paper
When: On a Thursday during the New Moon

Thursday is Jupiter's day, the planet in astrology that represents expansion, and expansion is what you're attempting to do with this spell. Place the gold candle at the northern end of your altar, the direction that represents, among other things, fertility. On the piece of paper, write: I embrace all opportunities for expanding my financial base. Place the piece of paper in front of the candle and put the quartz crystal on top of it. The crystal acts as a magnifier of your thoughts.

Light the candle, and visualize new financial opportunities flowing into your life. Read aloud what you have written down. Then burn the paper, releasing the desire. Let the candle burn down and toss it out.

As always, give thanks for the prosperity you already have.

A Spell to Increase Your Cash and Prosperity Flow

Tools:
12 plants with purple blooms
When: Whenever you feel the need

In feng shui, purple, violet, and lavender are associated with wealth and prosperity. Standing at your front door, locate the farthest left-hand corner of your home. That's your prosperity area. Put your plants in that room, if it has enough light. If it doesn't, place the plants as close as possible to that room.

A Quick Spell for Prosperity

One of the most frequent complaints people have about casting spells is that they take so much time. So here's a sixty-second spell to increase your general prosperity.

Tools:
Any purple, violet, or lavender object
Piece of paper and a pen
When: Whenever you feel the need, but most powerful on New Moon

Jot down the specific things you're trying to create in terms of prosperity. Tuck the list under the purple object, and make it so.

A Spell to Deflect Negative Energy

Take any reflective surface (pieces of aluminum foil or small mirrors, for example), and put them under the light of a midday sun (symbolically this turns away all darkness), saying:

Negativity away,
Darkness away,
Banished by the light of day!

Put these items in every window of your home, and make sure each one is facing outward.

A Spell to Attract Luck

Tools:
A coin minted in the year of your birth
A cabbage leaf
Ribbon or string
Natural fiber cloth

If you can, use a coin with high silver or gold content. Wrap the coin in the cabbage leaf (a good-luck food), and tie the bundle with the ribbon or string to bind the energy (choose the color of the string to correspond with your "lucky" or power color). Leave the cabbage leaf where it will naturally dry without molding (preferably during a Waxing Moon cycle so that luck "grows"). When it is completely dry, wrap it in the cloth and carry it with you regularly.

Create Your Own Lucky Charm

To make this, you'll need to find a coin minted in the year of your birth (or in a year that has special significance for you, like the year you discovered Wicca). If this can be a coin with a high silver content, all the better; silver is a metal aligned with the moon and the energy of good fortune. Empower the coin for luck by repeating the following incantation:

By word, will, and this silver coin,
Magick and fortune herein join!

Carry the coin with you or place it where you need the most luck.

A Mail Spell for Prosperity

Tools:
A $5 bill
Yellow construction paper

This spell is based on the threefold law. Take the money and wrap it the construction paper saying:

Return to me
By the law of three.

Mail this off anonymously to someone you know who is in need of a little extra cash. This spell usually yields a $15 return within three weeks.

A Fetish to Fight Bad Luck

We've all run into streaks of bad luck. Whip up a few of these fetishes, and you'll neatly disperse that negative energy.

Tools:
Three pennies
Three pieces of loosely woven cloth (in your lucky color)
Three pieces of white string

Use the string to tie each of the pennies into the cloth while reciting an incantation:

In luck I trust, in luck I believe,
Within this bundle, protection weave!

When you want to activate the fetish, take it to a remote location and put it into the earth, saying:

Bad fortune's come, but not to stay.
I command it now to turn away.

Turn away from the bundle and don't look back, leaving all that negative energy behind you.

Affirmations for Prosperity

The power of affirmations can't be emphasized too strongly, particularly in the area of prosperity and abundance. Even if you don't believe in the power of words, if you say something enough times, your unconscious mind begins to believe it and your reality begins to shift.

✦ **Wiccan Wonderings: When doing spells for prosperity, does it take away someone else's prosperity?**
Not at all. Prosperity and abundance don't have limits. You may have trouble, however, if you're casting spells to win the lottery or at gambling, or if you're attempting to swindle someone out of money. ✦

It can work for things both simple and grand. Are you waiting for a check that hasn't arrived? Then fifty times a day, repeat, "My check is here," or "My check arrives." Or perhaps you need extra money this month for renovations on your home. In this instance, you might say, "I have enough money to do the renovations."

Try not to concern yourself with *how* you're going to get that extra money. Simply be aware that opportunities will begin to present themselves to you if you continue to say the affirmation. Be alert for patterns of coincidence, which can serve as signposts to new opportunities. And *always* phrase your affirmation in the present tense!

Chapter 10

Spells for Lean Times

WE ALL GO THROUGH lean periods from time to time, and they aren't just financial. They can happen in any area of life or several areas at once. Your spouse loses a job. One of your parents dies. Your screenplay doesn't sell, your marriage falls apart, you develop a health problem. No matter where you turn, bad stuff happens.

Why the Lean Times?
The simple answer is, that's life—it isn't always a great, magnificent adventure. Sometimes it hurts. Sometimes, in fact, it's so painful we just want to curl up and sleep for as long as it takes the bad time to pass. Most of the time, in lean cycles, what's happening is so far beyond our immediate comprehension that all we can do is simply get through it.

Lean times seem to be cyclic for many people, but with awareness and applied intent, the pattern can be broken. Do your lean times seem to happen during a particular time of the month or year? Do the cycles seem to be connected to the phases of the moon or to the summer or winter solstice? Do things usually pick up for the better near or right after your birthday?

Using your birthday as a starting point, it's possible to plot your personal cycles by dividing the year into quarters. The first three months after your birthday tend to be a productive, busy time. You're

141

actively involved in the outer world, there are many demands on your time and energy, but things get done.

The second three months are still productive, but less active. This is a good time to assess what you've been doing in the last three months and to fine-tune.

The third quarter, beginning six months from your birthday, is usually a time of harvest. You're reaping the benefits of that first three months. You feel prosperous.

The fourth quarter—beginning about three months before your birthday—can be stressful. You may find that you tire more easily, that you're more irritable. If little things that go wrong during this period aren't fixed, they tend to become bigger problems.

You should be able to recognize a pattern in your quarterly cycles. As you work with them, other patterns may emerge.

Spells to Initiate Each Cycle

The Birthday Spell: Cycle 1

On or close to your birthday, set aside a few minutes to write down what you would like to have happen in the next three months. Be specific, read it aloud, then post it where you will see it frequently—on the door of the fridge, your bathroom mirror, next to your computer.

Every time you read what you've written, feel that reality around you. You can also create a charm or find a power totem that represents your desire and carry it with you. After you feel comfortable with what you've written—several days, a few weeks, whatever it takes—burn the paper, thus releasing your desire.

On your birthday, do something special for yourself to celebrate the beginning of a new annual cycle.

Spell for Cycle 2

On or around the date that marks the beginning of the second cycle, do what you did in the birthday spell. Since your energy during this period may be lower, light two red candles before you read aloud what you've written. After several days or weeks, burn the sheet of paper.

Plot Your Cycles

To plot your yearly cycles, jot notes about major events that happened during each quarterly period. Include details about how you felt. If you can't remember that far back, then begin with your most recent birthday and carry it through the year to your next birthday. ✦

Spell for Cycle 3

On or around the date that the third cycle begins, write down, as before, what you want for this period. This is your harvest period, so light a gold candle to represent continued prosperity and a violet candle to represent your gratitude for all the good things that have come your way.

Spell for Cycle 4

On or around the date that marks the beginning of the fourth cycle, follow what you did at the beginning of the three previous cycles. Light a red, gold, and violet candle, then read aloud what you've written.

On the day when this period begins, do something special for yourself and extend yourself to someone else by doing a good deed.

Fear

One of the biggest challenges we face during lean times is that old devil, fear. Fear can cripple the best intentions, squash the most buoyant spirit, and make a lean cycle a permanent condition.

It's difficult to imagine that you're prosperous or successful when you're unemployed and have $12 left in the bank. It's difficult to imagine yourself in a happy relationship when you're alone and feeling miserable. Difficult, but not impossible. Several breathing techniques can override fear, at least temporarily, and while the fear is at a low ebb, imagination can be employed to work through the fear and move beyond it.

Birthday Affirmation

As your birthday approaches, post this affirmation where you can see it frequently. The day after your birthday, toss the affirmation out, thus releasing it: "I trust that I am on a path to abundance and happiness, of gratitude and prosperity. I am peaceful, calm, filled with the certainty that all my days, from this day forward, are rich and splendid." ✦

Another way to break through the barrier of fear is as you're waking up in the morning. When you're still in that between state, not quite awake and not quite asleep, state your fear in a simple sentence. Draw an imaginary box around it. Light a match and set the imaginary box on fire. Sweep the imaginary ashes out the imaginary front door of your house.

As soon as you've done this, replace the statement about your fear with a positive affirmation. If, for instance, your fear is about debt or not having enough money, then some possibilities for positive affirmations might be:

- I have plenty of money.
- Money flows into my life from expected and unexpected sources.
- My life fills with abundance.
- I am rich.

As always, state your affirmation in the present tense and back it with emotion.

The place between sleep and wakefulness is an especially powerful state of consciousness for doing belief work. If you do it in the morning before you get out of bed, you're setting the tone for the day.

If you do it at night as you're falling asleep, your unconscious works on it. If you cling to your fear—or it clings to you—your lean times may linger because like attracts like.

Breaking the Fear Barrier

The next time fear is staring you in the face, don't turn around and run. Stare back. Confront it by asking yourself: *What is the absolute worst that can happen? What is this fear really saying to me?*

Here are a few tips for beating your fears:

- **Identify your fear:** If you don't identify your fears, they will unnecessarily spill into other areas of your life. Instead recognize the bottom line, or true root, of your fears. Once you do, you can come to a better understanding of your fears and start to move past them.
- **Release your fear:** When confronted with a fear, try finding an object to represent your fear, then take a hammer to it, and smash it. Physical exercise sometimes serves the same purpose. When you find yourself in the grip of fear, head for the outdoors, if you can, and walk fast. Better yet, run. Run until your legs ache and you're panting for breath.
- **Work through it:** Sometimes in life, certain situations are so painful or difficult that nothing seems to work to break the hold a particular fear has on you. In that case, you simply have to keep working with it and live through it day by day, until you can finally get past it.

Getting Through Lean Times

In lean times, draw on every tool and resource that you have—spells, affirmations, and visualization; dreams and oracles; power totems; colors; everything discussed so far in this book. In addition, you have to take action in the ordinary world—network with friends, and accept emotional support from friends, family, and any groups to which you belong. Recognize that it's okay to depend on others when you have to, especially when that support is offered.

In lean times, it's helpful to take stock of what is working in your life rather than focusing on what you don't have or what isn't working. Instead of bemoaning what's happened, try to look at it as an opportunity.

✳ Wiccan Wonderings: What do lean times teach us, anyway?

During lean times, it can be helpful to try to identify what you're supposed to be learning from the experience. If you're in debt, what are you learning about how to manage your money, or about the monetary value of your skills and talents? If you're lonely, what is your loneliness teaching you? Quite often, if you understand the lesson, whatever it is, the problem begins to ease. ✦

If you've lost your job, consider it as an opportunity to redirect your life toward work that is more satisfying. If your marriage has fallen apart, consider it an opportunity to get to know yourself as an individual rather than as half of a pair. If you didn't get the job you wanted, didn't sell your screenplay or novel, didn't land an account you went after, there may be reasons you can't see yet. At times, we may glimpse the bigger picture of our lives, but usually we don't live in that big picture.

If you can't see the opportunity, then pretend. You'll eventually trick yourself into believing it's true. If you live with the trick long enough, it will become your belief.

These five "attitude adjustments" will help you navigate lean times more easily:

Use all your resources.
Focus on what is working in your life.
Use adversity as opportunity.
Don't resist change; try to go with the flow.
Trust the process—we rarely have the full picture.

Lean Time Affirmations

During lean times, we all need a little extra help staying positive. Try these affirmations to help keep your chin up. Write or type them out and post them where you see them frequently.

1. I am now pulling in abundance and happiness.
2. My life is filled with great experiences.
3. I am grateful for all that I have.
4. I heal daily.
5. I give love freely.
6. I forgive and release.
7. I am moving forward with love and trust.

A Spell to Perpetuate Positive Energy

If you've hit a particularly rough spot in life, and optimism is in short supply, try this spell for a boost.

>   *Tools:*
>   Music that lifts your mood
>   Eucalyptus oil (healing)
>   Frankincense oil (psychic awareness)
>   Bay oil (love spells)
>   Jasmine (to sweeten the pot)
>   1 amber-colored candle
>   1 pink candle
>   1 orange candle
>   1 red candle
>   *When:* The New Moon

The New Moon is best for this spell because you're planting new seeds in your life. But you can do this spell on any night, whenever you need a boost of positive energy. After you have done it once, you can cast the spell in an abbreviated form during the day, simply through the power of fragrance.

With your intent firmly in mind, put on your favorite uplifting music and mix the oils in your burner. Light the candle in your burner so the fragrance of the oils thickens in the air. Select a candle that feels right to you and place it in the north. Then, moving in a clockwise direction, put the remaining candles at each of the cardinal points. Now move around the Circle, lighting each candle and saying:

> *I enter the flow of All That Is.*
> *I am filling with loving kindness.*
> *I forgive and I release*
> *And I draw*
> *The best to me,*
> *So mote it be.*

As you work with this spell, change the wording to fit your needs. Don't get locked into a rigid way of doing this.

While you're doing this spell, "fold" your wish or desire into your thoughts and feelings. Remember, the thought and the feeling are two parts of a whole. One without the other will work, but it will probably take longer, and it might not work as well as the two together. Once you find a way of casting this spell that works for you, don't be afraid to use it whenever you feel the need.

Chapter 11

Spells for Personal Power

PERSONAL POWER HAS a lot to do with having *presence*. To have it, you don't need to be a movie star, writer, politician, celebrity, or anyone else in the public eye. In fact, your job or career really has nothing to do with it. This type of presence comes from within. There are kids who have *it*. There are elderly people who have *it*. You can encounter people from all walks of life who have *it* and, quite often, they don't even realize what they have. In some instances, a person may be born with presence, but usually it's something that must be cultivated, nurtured, explored. Usually, it's an ineffable quality that manifests over time, with the development of self-knowledge.

There it is again. That old adage. *Know thyself.*

To know yourself and to use what you learn requires an act of will. The dictionary definition of the word describes it as "choice, determination, volition." But what does any of that really mean?

The Power of Your Will

Your *will* is the crux of every visualization, manifestation, and spell. It's the act of galvanizing yourself at the deepest levels to achieve something that you desire. You don't simply say the words. You don't just go through the motions. You plunge into yourself, you delve, to discover your true motives, needs, and desires. You work to bring that self-knowledge to full consciousness, into your daily awareness. Then you commit to the path and trust the process.

✳ **Wiccan Wonderings: What's the best way to build your store of personal power?**

To increase your personal power, first pinpoint which area of your life lacks power. Is it your professional life, love life, spiritual life, family life, or creative life? Once you determine which area you want to work on, redesign the Spell for Personal Empowerment to fit your needs. Refer to the material on ingredients, to decide what to use in your spell. Do this spell during the Full Moon. ✦

When you develop this sort of awareness, synchronicities tend to proliferate in your life and they often occur in clusters. More and more frequently, you may find that external events precisely mirror inner conditions. At the same time, your dreams might become especially vivid and cluster around one or two themes. Pay attention to these types of themes, as they are meant to help crystalize things and increase your understanding.

The spells that follow are intended to expand self-awareness and to enhance your will power.

A Spell to Expand Self-Awareness

Tools:
Frankincense oil
Myrrh oil
1 amber-colored candle
Object that represents personal power
Quartz crystal
When: Preferably on a Thursday night during a Full Moon

Thursday is Jupiter's day and Jupiter symbolizes expansion. If you can't do it on a Thursday, then definitely do this during a Full Moon, on any day except Tuesday (Mars) or Saturday (Saturn).

The object should be something solid and three-dimensional: a stone, for instance, versus a photograph. The crystal can be any color, but should be clear. It will amplify your desire.

Pick a spot where you won't be disturbed. If it's temperate where you are, this spell works nicely outside, under the light of the Full Moon. Put several drops of both oils into your burner and place it on your left. Put the amber-colored candle on your right. The object that represents your personal power and the crystal should go directly in front of you.

Light the candles, then throw open your arms to the moon. Vividly imagine its light suffusing you and say:

> *This light is presence,*
> *This light is power.*
> *It fills me*
> *Until I am presence,*
> *Until I am power.*

Allow the aroma of the oils to permeate the air, then pinch out the flames. Place your power object in a safe place. You may want to let your crystal soak in salt water overnight to cleanse it. Or, you can leave it outside, where the light of the Full Moon will charge it.

A Spell for Sexual Charisma

Tools:
Rue, the herb
Sage, incense or herb
Mint
4 candles, your choice of colors
When: Preferably a Tuesday or a Thursday on a Full Moon. If neither of those days is possible, then a Friday or Sunday would be fine, too.

As an herb, rue strengthens willpower, sage is excellent for mental clarity and protection and a general cleansing of negative energy, and mint speeds up the results of a spell. You can also consult the lists of herbs in this book and add any others that you feel are appropriate. Tuesday is ruled by Mars, which governs sexual energy. Jupiter, as Thursday's ruler, means expansion, luck.

If you're casting this spell in the hopes of seducing someone, then one of the candle colors should be red. Allow your intuition to guide you on the other three colors.

Light your herbs first, so their scent permeates the air where you're working. Next, light the candles. As you light each one, imagine your sexuality and your charisma burning brightly during the time that you need it to do whatever you're going to do!

The Flow

The flow is one of the millennial buzzwords and usually has "go with" preceding it, as in *Go with the flow.*

The biggest problem with this phrase is that it implies passivity. It seems to be saying that if we don't do anything, if we just wait for things to unfold, we're going with the flow. In actuality, the flow is like a current made up of synchronicities. It's up to us to figure out what these often odd connections mean, what their deeper significance is, and in doing so, we're able to determine the direction and purpose of the flow. This in itself is empowering. We feel as if we're hooked into something larger than ourselves, that the *bigger picture* is vastly more complex than we dared imagine.

The flow of a river is altered constantly by the curvature of the land that contains it, weather patterns, and myriad other environmental details. In the same way, the purpose of *the flow* in our lives changes as our goals and needs change. By developing an awareness of this deeper stratum of our lives, we're better equipped to anticipate opportunities, to deal with challenges, and to fulfill our potential. In short, we are empowered.

A Spell for Personal Empowerment

This spell requires no tools except the belief that magick works—and that it can work for you. As you're waking up in the morning, before your eyes open, when you're still in that drowsy state halfway between dreams and full consciousness, visualize whatever it is that you desire. Then say it silently to yourself.

Maybe your desire is to ace an exam. Visualize it as vividly as possible, a big red A at the top of your exam sheet. Pour emotion into it. Imagine how excited you'll be when you see the A. Then say, "I ace my exam." Again, put emotion behind the statement.

When you've done this with great vividness and backed it with emotions, then get out of bed and forget about it. Release the desire. Assuming that you've done your part to get an A on the exam (studied or otherwise prepared yourself), you should get an A.

This spell can be done quickly and can be done anywhere—not just as you're waking up in the morning. The most important ingredients are the vividness with which you visualize the end result and the intensity of the emotion behind your desire.

Your Field of Energy

Chinese medical practitioners call it *chi*. Hindu mystics refer to it as *shakti*. Medical intuitives call it an *energy field*. Occultists refer to it as an *aura*. Its existence has been recorded since ancient times, notably in primitive art. In the Sahara desert, for instance, in the rocky massifs of that harsh terrain, paintings that date back to the ninth millennium B.C. show human figures surrounded by an envelope of light. In Catholic literature, these luminous orbs are depicted as halos.

This energy field ". . . is an intuitive language of the body," writes Judith Orloff, M.D., in *Judith Orloff's Guide to Intuitive Healing.* "It is the essence of who we are, a subtle vibration underlying everything physical, both living and inanimate . . . some of us may see it more easily . . . others may feel it."

The energy field radiates outward from the body, forming a dome of light that can be several inches or several feet wide, depending on the individual's emotional, spiritual, and physical state at any given time. It's composed of at least seven energy disks or chakras that run down the center of the physical body, from the crown of the head to the base of the spine. Each of these chakras has a different color and function, which are important to medical intuitives. More on the energy field and energy centers is provided in the chapter on health spells. For the spells in this chapter, however, the colors and the function of each energy center are the most important elements.

Energy Centers and Corresponding Colors

Chakra	Color	Function	Location
First	Red	Survival	Genitals
Second	Orange	Sexuality, nurturing	Below navel
Third	Yellow	Emotions, power	Solar plexus
Fourth	Green	Compassion, love	Between nipples
Fifth	Blue	Communication	Throat
Sixth	Purple	Intuition, intellect	Between eyes
Seventh	White	Spirituality, knowledge	Crown of head

Let's say that you're going to be interviewing for a job that seems absolutely ideal for you. Great hours, great flexibility, the whole nine yards. But you're nervous about the interview, uncertain about what to say or how to say it. A spell to enhance and empower your throat chakra might be just what you need to get through the interview with flying colors.

Perhaps you're having trouble with a boss at work. You're unable to claim your rightful power because the boss intimidates you. A spell for the solar plexus chakra may be just the ticket to resolve the problem.

The idea here is that by focusing on the appropriate areas of your energy field, you're delivering a double whammy of empowerment.

A Spell for Empowering the Energy Centers

For the first energy center:

Tools:
4 red candles
When: A Friday night on the Full Moon

This spell is quick and simple. It only requires that you bring your intent and your belief to the spell.

Place the four candles at the four cardinal directions. Starting at the north, move clockwise to light the candles. With each candle that you light, imagine your first center as a swirling orb of strong, pulsating energy that imbues your being with sexual charisma and power.

When you have finished lighting the candles, spend a few minutes in the center of your candle Circle, preferably in the lotus position. Inhale deeply several times, then exhale quickly, expelling all the air from your lungs. Pinch your right nostril shut, inhale through the left, and hold to the count of ten. Exhale through the right nostril. Repeat five times and switch sides. As you do this alternate nostril breathing, imagine your first energy center imbued with power.

This spell can be repeated with each of the centers, using the appropriate colors. When you feel comfortable casting spells, you can create your own rhyme for each of the cardinal directions, to say when you light the candles.

Stretching Your Energy Field

People who have presence, who have personal power, often have an expanded energy field or aura as well. The energy field, in fact, is what we react to when that person walks into our view.

With practice, you can learn to expand your energy field from the usual several inches around your body to several feet. The field is easy to detect through touch. Stand in front of a mirror and open your arms wide, as if you're about to hug someone. Bring your hands slowly toward your head until you feel a slight resistance. This should happen when your hands are several inches away from your head. When your energy field expands, you'll feel the resistance farther away from your head.

You can also train yourself to see your energy field. Gaze into a mirror in a twilit room. It's best if a dim light is at your back. If you wear glasses or contacts, remove them. If you have 20/20 vision, gaze at your head in the mirror and let your eyes unfocus, so that your reflection seems hazy.

The longer you gaze at your reflection in this way, the more likely you are to see a halo of light surrounding your head. Some people detect colors, others simply see a halo of transparent light. Now think of something that made you exceptionally happy—your marriage, the birth of your child, the purchase of your first home, getting an offer for a great job. Conjure the emotions that you felt during this event or experience. Let the emotion fill you completely. As the emotions suffuse your entire being, your energy field will start to expand, and the halo will balloon.

As you're feeling your energy field expand, take several deep breaths. Pinch your right nostril shut and breathe in through your left nostril. Hold your breath to the count of ten and exhale through your right nostril. Repeat three times, then switch nostrils. Alternate nostril breathing stimulates both hemispheres of the brain and, as you become accustomed to charging your energy field, the alternate breathing signals your unconscious of your intent.

With practice, you can charge your energy field in ten or fifteen seconds. You can use this technique for just about anything—when you're hoping to attract love, new job opportunities, or meet new friends. Your body becomes the tool. It can be done anywhere, anytime.

Chapter 12

Spells for Creativity

IN ITS BROADEST DEFINITION, "creativity" is the act of coming up with something new rather than producing an imitation. We tend to think of creativity as applying only to certain areas of life, such as arts or inventions, but in reality, creativity belongs to all aspects of life.

All of us are inherently creative. We all come up with new ways of doing things, new ideas, new approaches, new perspectives and insights. Our right brains are tireless workers. They churn out ideas twenty-four hours a day, every day, every year of our lives. Part of our problem, however, is that we're creatures of habit. If something has worked in the past, we keep following that groove because it takes less effort—and besides, who wants to mess with success? We begin to approach living from some sort of internal formula. If we do A, then we do B and C all the way through Z, even though it might feel old and tired. Then we sit up one day and realize with a certain growing horror that we have fallen into a rut.

If you feel like you're in a rut, use the following brainstorming questions as a springboard to provide insight into your own creative process, what you need to alter to become more creative, and what your ultimate creative goals are.

1. If you could do anything with your life, what would it be?
2. What are your hobbies, and why?

3. Do you consider your hobbies creative? Why or why not?
4. Do you consider yourself creative?
5. What do you consider the most creative part of your life and why?
6. Do you feel as if you're in a rut in any area of your life? If so, are you willing to change it?
7. Describe your rut.
8. What do you think you can do to change it? If it's a job, are you willing to change jobs? If it's a relationship, are you willing to reassess it or get out of it?
9. What's the first step you would take to get out of the rut?
10. How can you apply your creative talents in another area of your life to get out of that rut?

Breaking Out of Your Rut

Let's say you're stuck in a rut at work. You hate your job but at the moment, you don't have any other prospects on the horizon. Even so, you're preparing a résumé, putting out feelers, and setting things in motion. In the meantime, you can do some simple magick, and it starts with nothing more than taking a different route to and from work.

On the first morning that you take the new route, give yourself some extra time. Leave ten or fifteen minutes earlier than usual. Notice how this route to work differs from the one you ordinarily take. Is it more scenic? More hectic? Is it longer or shorter? Take note of any feelings you have during the drive, any thoughts and insights that surface.

Throughout your day at work, notice if you feel differently about your job. Are you more committed to finding something else to do? Are your thoughts any clearer? Does your boss still rub you the wrong way?

Even by changing something as minor as this, you're breaking out of your habitual ways of doing things. Once you change your drive to work, you can start doing other small, routine tasks in your work and home life differently. Changing old patterns and ways of thinking serves as a symbolic gesture to the universe that you're ready for change. Never underestimate the power of change—with new dreams, you can create a new life.

✳ **Wiccan Wonderings: What, exactly, is a creative muse, and how can you get in touch with it?**

The creative muse is nearly always spoken of as "she." But a muse can also be a "he" or have no gender at all. It can simply be energy that you name, as you might a beloved pet. To get in touch with your muse, simply put out the request: Write it in your journal; tell yourself as you're falling asleep that you're going to communicate with your muse in a dream; meditate on it; or even write your muse a note. ✦

A Spell to Change Outmoded Patterns

Once you've identified the patterns you want to change in your life, make one small gesture that expresses your intent. Then, on the first night of the Full Moon, jot down your desire on a sheet of paper, in ink of a color that seems appropriate for what you want. For instance, if your wish is to be more creative with your financial investments, then use green ink. Or, if you want to be more creative in your professional life, use gold ink. Then light two candles of a close or matching color and read your wish out loud three times. Back the words with emotion—say them as if you mean them. Tuck your written desire under a power object and let the candles burn out naturally.

On the second night of the Full Moon, light two more candles of the same color. Repeat your wish three times. Then touch the paper to one of the flames and say:

> *As this paper is burning,*
> *I release my wish, my need,*
> *My deepest yearnings,*
> *A new life's seed.*

When the second set of candles has burned out on its own, toss it out.

A Spell to Enhance Creativity

Choose something that represents the area of your life where you would like to enhance or increase your creativity. Any object or symbol will do. Keep it in a place where you'll see it daily. Every time you see it, think of *Star Trek* and use Captain Picard's slogan: "Make it so."

Feel the words as you think them. Feel your changing beliefs. Then, make a gesture that's connected to your creativity at least once a day for a month.

Creativity and Dreams

Dream books are filled with stories about how a dream provided the missing piece of an invention, vital scenes in a novel, the finishing touches of a movie, or some unique image in a painting. Dreams are so intimately connected to creativity and to the creative process that to ignore them or to write them off as merely pleasant interludes is to cheat yourself.

The fodder dreams provide comes to each of us in unique ways. Some dreams are symbolic, others are literal. Some are ordinary, others are bizarre. Some are fun, some are terrifying. Regardless of the particularities in which a dream is couched, it is *your* dream, intimately connected to the creative process that churns inside of you every day of your life.

Dreams are the conduit through which we connect to each other and to the deeper, oceanic parts of ourselves. Within that vast inner ocean are buried creative seeds that may never sprout unless we bring them into the light of day. Dreams, by their fundamental nature, are magick.

Here are a few guidelines on how to recall your dreams and work with them to enhance your creativity:

- **Voice what you need or want.** Before you fall asleep at night, say aloud that you would like to remember the most important dreams of the night. If you're trying to find a particular solution to something, then request that an answer come to you in a dream that you'll remember in detail.
- **Back up your request with a gesture.** Put a recorder by your bedside or slide a notebook under your pillow so that you can immediately record what you remember when you wake up. You might even jot your request on a page in your journal. Date it. Make notes the next day about whether you remembered any dreams. Sometimes the act of trying to write about your dreams when you're sure you haven't remembered any is enough to trigger recall.
- **Pay attention.** Any dream fragment that you remember may relate to your request even if it doesn't appear to do so. Don't judge it. Forget your left-brain censor. Just write down the fragment. Record it.
- **If you don't succeed at first, keep trying.** Yes, it's a cliché. It also happens to be true. If you've spent thirty or forty years forgetting the bulk of what goes on while you sleep, then you can bet the remembering wheels are rusty. Oil them and keep making your requests. Sooner or later, you'll have a powerful, significant dream, and you'll remember the characters, the texture, the nuances.
- **Experiment.** If you don't seem to be remembering any dreams or your requests don't appear to be working, then sleep elsewhere for a couple of nights. On the couch. In a sleeping bag. At your mother's place. When we break the rut we're in by changing a habit, new things unfold.

All of this might not sound like spell work, but it is. You are bringing your intent, will, emotions, and anything else you can muster to get a creative solution to your request. It's visualization in another form.

"My safest place is in my dreams," writes Judith Orloff in *Intuitive Healing*. "There I become centered. I inhabit a form that feels more fluid, and I effortlessly replenish myself with images, energy, tones that are a bigger stretch to accommodate otherwise."

Maybe that's the key. Each of us must befriend our dreams, must approach them as though they are old friends who will listen to us and offer a fresh perspective on whatever we're looking for or need.

A Spell to Bring about Vivid Dreams

Create a ritual for going to bed. Have a cup of chamomile tea, a glass of milk, or a bowl of ice cream beforehand. Treat yourself to a food or drink from which you derive comfort, the kind of comfort that your parents gave you when you were a kid, preparing to go to bed.

Place a sprig of vervain under your pillow, next to your dream journal or recorder—it promotes vivid dreams. So do the color blue, the scent of cedar (incense or oil), a warm bath, and the sound of water. A small fountain will do the trick and so will the gentle caress of the ocean surf against a beach. Sometimes, the whisper of wind is invaluable. Do something that soothes each of your senses.

As you get into bed, state your request. Spend a few minutes reading or doing whatever relaxes you. As you turn out the light, repeat your request, and trust that it will be answered.

Practical Creativity

This might sound like an oxymoron, but creativity is always practical. It's the perfect blend of right and left brain. What the right brain can conceive, the left brain can put into action.

If your creative impetus feel sluggish and you can't seem to get to first base with spells, dreams, or anything else, then maybe it's time to take a back-door approach and do some left-brain defining.

The creative process begs for a structure. *Give me a goal*, it pleads. *Give me a backbone. And if you can't do that, then at least give me a deadline.*

A deadline often provides the badly needed backbone for creativity. The advertising executive needs three spots for tomorrow's slot at 8 A.M. The reporter needs to call in his story at noon. The gallery needs two paintings for this week's exhibit. Forget dreams. Forget visualizations. Forget the tools that have worked before. You need a product and you need it *now*.

At such times, the creativity God slams into overdrive. It plucks up this remnant from sixth grade and that vague memory from the day your mother died and tosses in the color purple and a scent of pine. It squeezes all these seemingly disparate pieces into the backbone your left brain created and suddenly you have a product. You have an answer. You have a solution.

Left brain, right brain. The difference, on the surface, is nothing more than hemispheres and directions. The left brain, the experts tell us, is good at math and reasoning, good at minutia and connecting the dots. The right brain excels at seeing the whole picture. Neither is better than the other. We need both. We can't survive if the signal from one is very weak or very strong. *We need a balance between the two, and it doesn't matter which one takes the lead.* Creativity rises from a perfect blend between left brain and right.

A Spell to Balance the Hemispheres

Before you dive into a creative project, find a comfortable spot anywhere, shut the door, and sit on the floor, with your back against a wall. Hold your left nostril shut and breathe through the right. Hold it to the count of ten and exhale forcefully through your mouth. Repeat this three times, then switch sides and repeat three times.

This breathing exercise, used in certain yoga traditions, balances both hemispheres of the brain, allowing them to work smoothly together. It allows them to talk to each other. And that talk, that private conversation they have, is essential to any creative process.

Once you get the hang of it, you can do this breathing exercise anywhere, anytime.

Calling on Nature to Boost Creativity

What if you've tried all of that alternate breathing stuff, and you've worked at your dream recall, but nothing's panned out? You're still so entrenched in your rut that you can feel its walls collapsing around you.

Then it's time for a break. Put on your sneakers and head for the great outdoors. If you live in a large city, the outdoors might amount to not much more than a square foot of green or a park. In the suburbs, you might have a few more choices, and any of them will do the trick, but what I'm talking about here is the *real outdoors*. No conveniences within fifteen or twenty miles. No 7-Elevens, no gas stations, no shopping malls, no movie theaters. That's the best scenario. In lieu of that, find a green place that is moderately private.

Wild Animals and the Creative Spark

When we run across an animal in the wild, we are seized by an archetypal energy of freedom and instinct. Depending on the circumstances and the type of animal, we might be seized by fear as well. But even fear can galvanize our creativity. The vividness of even the briefest encounters with wild animals stays with you, and it can trigger all sorts of creative thoughts and images. ✦

Use what's available where you live. Get out, walk, hike, ride a horse—*just break your routine in a major way*. Observe the wildlife. Enjoy the smell of the air, the firmness of the ground under your feet. And take note of how your thought processes start to change. You'll have to put up with your internal grumblings at first. You know, the usual complaints: *It's too far, I'm hot, I'm thirsty, I'm hungry, Where's the bathroom*, and so on. But when you get past all that—and you will—something magickal happens. You can almost feel the inner shift.

Your thoughts begin to flow rather than to sputter. Your rhythm changes. Your gait quickens or slows. You feel lighter, happier, more optimistic. And this is exactly the right atmosphere for your creativity to percolate.

Quite often, when you venture into nature simply to see what you'll discover, your creativity is stimulated in unusual and, sometimes, enduring ways. When British biologist and author Rupert Sheldrake was a young boy, his father used to take him to see the freeing of homing pigeons that had come from all over Britain. "When the appointed time came, the porters opened the flaps and out burst hundreds of pigeons, batch after batch, in a great commotion of wind and feathers," he writes in *Seven Experiments That Could Change the World*. His fascination with homing pigeons as a boy eventually led to the first experiment in his book many decades later.

A Practical Spell

Talk about creativity and animals, creativity and dreams, and creativity and nature is all well and good, but if you have a specific goal, you need to make it practical. Do you have a screenplay that needs to find its way to the right people? Paintings or photographs that deserve to be exhibited? Have you written the great American thriller? If so, try this spell to sell.

> *Tools:*
> Pen and paper
> Something that represents what you want to sell
> Any oil or incense whose scent makes you feel optimistic
> 3 candles—red, gold, and violet
> *When:* Three consecutive nights, beginning with the Full Moon

The item you choose to represent what you want to sell is especially important in this spell. If, for instance, you're a realtor and are trying to sell a particular house or property, then you might choose a little house or a hotel from a Monopoly game to represent the property. If you want to sell a manuscript or screenplay, then perhaps a book or a video can serve as a symbol. On a piece of paper, write your desire in present tense. *My screenplay sells quickly.* Or: *The Smith house sells quickly.* Slip this under the item that symbolizes your desire.

Light the oil or incense. As you light the red candle, say your desire out loud three times. The red brings energy into your desire. Let the candle and the incense burn out naturally. Leave the vestiges of the red candle on your altar or wherever you do the spell.

What Our Pets Teach Us about Creativity

Anyone who has pets recognizes their roles in our creativity. They are part of the natural world that we bring indoors, into our lives. Once we invite them in and they accept the invitation, our lives invariably change. If we're lucky, our cats teach us how to laze in the sun with our bellies to the sky, so immersed *in the moment* that the rest of the world goes away. And although we might not be able to smell what our dogs smell in the summer grass, we can learn that same focus by watching them. ✦

On the second night, repeat this ritual but light the gold candle. It represents your desire for success. Let the candle and incense burn out and leave the spent gold candle next to the red one. On the third night, light the purple candle. The purple symbolizes your highest good. When it burns out, toss out all three candles, releasing your desire.

A Spell to Sell a Book—or Any Other Creative Product

This spell comes from June, Lady Ciaran, to her coven.

> *Tools:*
> Basil
> Cinnamon
> 1 yellow taper candle (pink will do, but yellow is best)
> Pen to write anything on the contents of the envelope or to
>   address the envelope
> *When:* During the Waxing Moon (New Moon to first quarter)

Using the pen, inscribe the name of your book, with arrows pointing to it (up and down) into the candle. Figure out your lucky book number. To do this, take the number of pages in your book and add the digits together. If, for example, your book has 256 pages, then add 2 + 5 + 6. The outcome is your lucky book number. Light the candle and chant the following as many times as your lucky book number.

My book/product, _____ (name of book/product), is the one I'm
    sending off.
I've worked and slaved over it. Please let my talent be enough.
Please let the publisher (agent) read/use/watch it and love it.
By the power of this candle I have lit,
So Mote It Be!

Chapter 13

Spells for Business

THE QUALITY OF YOUR professional life is intimately connected with your beliefs about prosperity and success. If you feel unworthy, this will be reflected in your pocketbook and in your work. If, on the other hand, you believe you're deserving—of a raise, a promotion, of better working conditions—this will also be reflected in your life.

In the following brainstorming activity, you're going to take inventory of your professional life—the work you do, your bosses and the people who have power over you, your coworkers or employees, or your personal professional circumstances if you're self-employed.

If you work for someone else:
1. Describe the work that you do, using specific details.
2. Is your work satisfying? Why or why not?
3. Do you get along with your boss?
4. Do you get along with your coworkers?
5. Are you passionate about your work?
6. What would you change about your work if you could?
7. Do you have moral or ethical objections to the work you do?
8. Do you feel you're paid fairly for what you do?
9. What are your professional goals for the next year? The next five years?
10. Do you have regrets about the professional path you've chosen?

11. Have you gotten regular promotions and raises? If not, why?
12. Is your work life filled with power struggles? If so, explain.

If you are self-employed:
1. What type of service do you provide?
2. Do you have employees? If so, how many?
3. Do you like most of your employees? Do they do a good job? If not, explain.
4. What would you like to change about your business and why?
5. Do you consider yourself a fair boss?
6. Are you earning enough for what you do?
7. What are your professional goals for the next year? The next five years?
8. If you could choose to do anything you wanted, what would it be? Why?
9. Are you passionate about what you do?
10. If your passions lie elsewhere, can you imagine earning your living at it?

If your answers to the above questions are primarily positive, then you're probably exactly where you want to be in life right now. If the answers are predominantly negative, keep them in mind as you read the chapter.

Spells and Goals

Setting goals is intrinsic to professional achievement. The goals don't have to be set in stone, but it's important to have a bigger picture in mind concerning what you would like to accomplish professionally.

Whether you want to change professions or jobs, or to simply move ahead in the profession or job you presently have, setting goals helps you clarify what you want. Once you know what you're after, it's easier to use the proper spells.

Write down your goals for three specific periods of time—you can select the time divisions that work for you. If you're an impatient person, make the increments small—a few days, six weeks—so that you can see your progress quickly. If you've got the patience of a saint, you can extend the increments out over a larger chunk of time.

A Spell for Clarification

This spell is intended to clarify a goal that you have. Quite often, we think we want one thing only to find later that what we wanted was something else entirely. So before you get to that "later on" point, do this simple spell for clarification.

> *Tools:*
> A few drops of cedar oil
> Pen and paper
> *When:* As you feel the need

Put the drops of cedar oil in your burner and light it. As the scent suffuses the air, write down your goal. Keep it simple. Now shut your eyes and sit quietly for a few moments with your goal in mind. Imagine that you have achieved this goal. How does it feel? Are you comfortable with it? How do your family and friends act toward you? What is your life like now that you have attained what you wanted?

The more vivid and detailed your imaginings, the greater benefit you derive from this visualization. Do this as long as you can keep imagining vividly, then stop. Now read your goal again. Is it what you really want? If not, rewrite it. You may find that you merely need to fine-tune what you've written.

If you rewrite your goal, let it sit for a day or two before you look at it again. Then ask yourself if it feels right. Chances are, it will.

New Ventures

A new job, a new profession, a new lease on your professional life—all of these things fall in this category.

Nothing can be as frightening as the prospect of starting something new. We worry about whether we should give it a whirl. We worry about whether we're young enough, experienced enough, or talented enough to make a go of it. We worry because we've been conditioned to worry, to berate ourselves, to assume we don't have what it takes.

A young writer once wrote a book, didn't think it was good enough to be published, and tossed it in the garbage. His wife retrieved the manuscript and it was not only published, it became a bestseller and a movie. The author? Stephen King. The book? *Carrie.*

Back in the early 1980s, a young woman had an idea about color and skin tones. But she didn't know how to put it together. On a

Business Charm

A charm is basically the Western equivalent of a shaman's medicine bundle. It should be small enough to carry with you, yet large enough to accommodate the objects you put inside. A charm for business power should be made of cotton or silk, and the color should represent the chakra you use most frequently in your work. If you do a lot of talking in your job, then blue might be the best color for the bag because blue represents the throat chakra, the center of your expression. If your job entails counseling, then the cloth might be a mixture of blue for expression and green to represent the compassion of the heart chakra. (If you're unsure about what color to use, consult the color list in Chapter 4.)

Keep the number of objects in your bundle to a minimum, and be sure the items symbolize something important to you. You can also put slips of paper with your desires or needs written on them in your bundle. From time to time, cleanse the items in your bundle by washing them in sea salt and charging them in the sun. If they can't be washed, simply set them outside in the sun for a few minutes. As your charm works its magick on particular projects or issues, consider replacing the items with other objects.

plane trip, she happened to sit next to a young man and told him her idea. He became second in command, she became the CEO, and the company was called Color Me Beautiful.

Sometimes, it takes another person to recognize our genius and help us organize it.

A Spell to Recognize Your Genius

This spell is intended to attract the individual who recognizes your genius and helps you pull together your vision of what might be, whatever that vision is.

Tools:
Seeds for a plant that has round leaves or purple flowers
Ceramic pot
Potting soil
When: Thursday during a Waxing Moon

Fill your ceramic pot with potting soil and place nine seeds at various points in the soil. As you plant the seeds, say aloud:

As I plant these seeds
I draw to me
The one who sees
What I can be.
So mote it be.

Once the seeds begin to sprout, the person who recognizes your genius should appear in your life. Until that happens, keep the plant in the northern section of your home—the place for career. Or, if that isn't possible, locate the wall or section of your house that is directly opposite your front door. If you have a particular room in your house where you do most of your work, the pot could also go in there, along the wall opposite the door or along the northern wall.

A Spell to Enhance Magnetism

This spell helps on that first day in a new job, with a new boss, new coworkers, new ventures, and professional situations.

Tools:
1 red candle
1 violet candle
1 quartz crystal
Your favorite oil
When: Waxing moon

This spell enhances your aura and fills it with magnetism that attracts what you need. It also protects you from what you don't need. The quartz crystal amplifies the magnetism.

Light your burner and as the scent suffuses the air, inhale deeply, and light the red candle. Say aloud:

The magnetism of this red flame
Enters me by name,
(say your name)
So mote it be.

Light the violet candle and say:

The protection of this violet flame
Enters me by name
(say your name)
So mote it be.

Let the candles burn out naturally. Bury them in your yard or in a flower pot, so the power stays with you always.

Mitigating Negative Situations

Most of us have bad days now and then at work. Occasionally, however, a bad day collapses into a really negative situation. Then it's more difficult to get back on the right track because it seems we're bogged down by negativity.

✳ **Wiccan Wonderings: How do you find the right amulet for business power?**

An amulet isn't something you can look for. It comes to you, it appears, it falls off a shelf at your feet. It can be any object that resonates with you. The actual object matters less than the sentiment you attach to it. It simply must be something that speaks to you, and when you first see it, you know it's yours. This applies to amulets for business, love, travel, or anything else. ◆

In situations like this, the longer you dwell on what went wrong, the worse it looks and the more negative and bleak your outlook becomes. It's one of those self-perpetuating cycles. To break the cycle and mitigate the negative situation, the first thing you have to do is step back and detach emotionally from whatever has happened. Remember that your point of power resides *in the moment*. You can't change what has happened, but you can alter your perspective about it and that, in turn, can soften the impact.

A Spell to Release Negativity

> *Tools:*
> 1 white candle
> 1 bay leaf
> White flowers, preferably carnations
> *When:* The Waning Moon

Power Symbols

An object is merely an object until it has, for lack of a better word, *soul*. That soul comes from the person who owns it, touches it, takes care of it, and in doing so, imbues that thing with the uniqueness of who he or she is. Objects absorb and reflect our energy, just by being in the same space that we inhabit. If we're passionate about something, that energy is heightened. It lingers, without any effort on our part. But when we consciously imbue an object with our passion, intent, and desires, then the object becomes extremely powerful. If you need a bit of power on your side to help you gain the upper hand in a business situation—or any situation—make sure that the objects around you are there for a purpose and not just for decoration.

If the situation is pressing, you can do this spell at any time. But any spell to release or cleanse is most powerful during the Waning Moon.

Place the bay leaf next to your vase of flowers and light your candle. Say aloud:

> *I now release (name the situation)*
> *and create new, positive energy to carry me forward.*
> *I trust this is for my highest good*
> *and affirm my commitment to this new path.*
> *I say so be it.*

Let the candles burn out on their own. Toss out the bay leaf with the flowers when they die.

A Point of Power Spell

With this spell, you're affirming that your point of power is in the present. The moment is your launching pad for the rest of your life. You can do this spell in conjunction with the previous spell or you can do it alone, for virtually any situation or issue.

Tools:
Ginger
Potted plant with yellow flowers
1 green candle
1 purple candle
Power object
When: Thursday or Friday during a Waxing Moon

With this spell, you're affirming in your own mind that your point of power is, indeed, in the present. Put the ginger between each of the candles and the vase of flowers behind the ginger. As you light the candles, say aloud:

My point of power,
like this plant that flowers,
some way, somehow
lies in the now.

Pinch out the candles when you're finished and toss out the ginger. Put the potted plant into the soil where you can see it. If it's not possible to plant it outside, then transplant it to a larger pot and put it in a window where you can see it.

A Spell to Get a Raise or Promotion
Do this spell only if you're convinced that you're worthy of a raise or a promotion. Otherwise, you're just saying words.

Tools:
2 gold candles
$20 bill that represents your raise
Sprig of sage
Pen and paper
When: During the Waxing Moon, preferably on a Thursday night

The bill you use to represent your raise can be of any denomination. It's merely a symbol.

Jot down what you would like your raise to be. Phrase it in the present tense and add "or better" at the end of it. Your statement might read: "I get a $5,000 raise or better." If you're doing this for a job promotion, jot it down in the same format.

Set the piece of paper and the bill between the gold candles. As you light the candles, say aloud:

> *Element of fire,*
> *Hear my desire,*
> *A raise (promotion) is due to me,*
> *(state what you want) or better,*
> *Make it so to the letter.*

Once you feel the rightness of what you're saying, once it *resonates* inside of you, then burn the piece of paper on which you wrote what you wanted, thus releasing the desire. Pinch out the flames and toss out the candles and the ashes of the sage.

A Spell for the Frequent Business Flyer

If you travel frequently on business, this spell can save you time, aggravation, and stress. Do this spell several hours before you leave for the airport.

Tools:
Several drops of amber or sandalwood oil
1 violet or purple candle
Sprig of sage
Pen and paper
When: As needed

On a sheet of paper, write: *My trip unfolds smoothly. I arrive safely and on time at my destination.* Set the paper next to the candle. Light the burner for the amber or sandalwood, then light the sage. Now light your candle and read what you've written out loud. Read it again silently and envision yourself at your destination, on time, with your bags, refreshed and at peace.

Read what you've written aloud once more, then burn it, releasing your desire. Blow or pinch out the candles and toss them out with the sage. Blow out the candle in the burner and give thanks that you are in a position to travel.

Chapter 14

Spells for Your Home

OUR HOMES MIRROR our feelings about where we live and whatever we've experienced while living in the house. This sounds obvious, until we're confronted with the profundity of what it actually means. Nowhere is the significance more apparent than when we see the reflections in other people's homes.

For most of us, our impressions about a house are probably formed the moment we walk in the front door. We immediately sense whether the place is friendly or hostile, chaotic or organized, formal or casual. We immediately like it or dislike it. Usually, our feelings don't have much to do with the furnishings or the color of the rugs, and they might not even be related to the layout of the rooms. We're reacting, instead, to a general overall impression, a *feeling tone*.

A Home's Unique Personality

In homes that aren't brand new, the feeling tone is something that has built up over a period of months or years. If the people who live in the house are predominately happy, we feel it. If tragedies have happened in the house, we feel that, too.

Houses, like people, carry emotional baggage. If you've ever gone house-hunting, you've probably noticed the feelings you pick up when you walk inside a house and through its rooms. It's almost as if the walls hold secrets, the floors whisper tales, and the porches laugh or weep.

Even new houses have a certain feeling tone. You can sense that everyone from the architects to the trade people has left their imprints on the rooms. Houses, apartments, duplexes—all of them speak to us. Even hotels have voices. The Overlook Hotel in Stephen King's classic *The Shining* has absorbed decades of emotions from the guests who have stayed there, and that emotional residue has taken on a life of its own. In a sense, that hotel is very much alive.

The same is true in Shirley Jackson's book *The Haunting of Hill House,* in Richard Matheson's novel *Stir of Echoes*, and in every similar story ever written or filmed. The difference between fiction and life, however, is that the energy that imbues a place isn't always bad. It's often uplifting, buoyant, and optimistic. It might even make us feel on top of the world as soon as we cross the threshold.

What is the feeling tone of the place where you live? Use the following "Brainstorming" exercise to find out:

1. Describe your home.
2. Describe how you feel about your home.
3. What would you change about where you live, and why?
4. Describe how you feel most of the time when you're at home.
5. Is your home spacious enough to accommodate everyone who lives in it comfortably?
6. Are the rooms cluttered?
7. Which areas or items in your home don't work or need attention? Think about your attic, basement, roof, doors, floors, walls, carpets, sinks and faucets, electrical outlets, and so on.
8. How do most people react to visiting your home?
9. Do you like your neighborhood? Why or why not?
10. Describe your dream house.
11. Why did you rent/lease/buy this place?
12. Overall, how would you describe your experiences in this house? Have you been predominantly happy, sad, or indifferent?

Analyzing Your Home

Question 7 is especially important because it helps to identify possible challenges and problems in your life right now. Look at the various listings as a metaphor. Let's say your garage door is stuck. It won't go up. If we look at the metaphor for what a garage door represents, perhaps you have trouble admitting new people and experiences into your life. Maybe you feel trapped. Maybe you don't know how to *open a door* to opportunity.

The answers to 8 and 12 might be similar. If your experiences in your home are predominately positive, that is probably what other people will feel. The reverse is also true. This doesn't mean that the *feeling tones* of a place are confined to either/or, good or bad, black or white. Quite often, we live in shades of gray. We walk the middle. We don't experience extremes. Our homes also absorb that.

With spells, we can protect, energize, and calm our homes. We can cleanse them of negative energy, boost their positive energy, ward off potential enemies or problems, and create atmospheres of success and happiness within their walls. We can make our homes easier to sell and we can cast spells to find the home of our dreams. In short, we can do for our homes and living spaces what we do for ourselves. The same rules apply. It's all about belief, intent, and desire.

A Spell to Get Rid of Negative Energy

Tools:
Sage, the herb (basil can be used as an alternative)
When: The Waning Moon

This ritual originates with Native Americans and is a popular method for cleansing just about anything.

When burned, sage is a sweet smelling herb. Some types smell like burning marijuana; others smell of summer in the great outdoors.

But the scent of the sage is less important than the cleansing properties of the sage itself.

To cleanse a room, simply pass the smoke of the burning sage over the walls, into the corners, the closets, any nooks and crannies where shadows—and energy—gather. Pass the smoke along the frames of the doors and windows. Let it eddy across the floor. This simple process is vital whenever something tragic, negative, or emotionally wrenching has happened. It's also beneficial if someone in your home is physically ill or feeling out of sorts.

You don't have to say anything or engage in any ritual. Simply hold the intent in your mind that you are cleaning the area of negative energy.

A sage wand is ideal for smudging. It doesn't have to be relit, it's easy to carry, and when you're finished, you simply stub out the burning end so that it can be used again.

The Waning Moon is the ideal time for this spell because you're *getting rid of something.* You're purging. You're doing the equivalent of a *limpieza,* or cleansing, in Santería.

A Spell to Invite Greater Happiness into Your Home

Tools:
Several round-leaf house plants
Violet- or lavender-scented incense or oil
Vase of freshly cut flowers
When: Any time

Inviting happiness into your home shouldn't be confined to a particular time of day or night, or even to any phase of the moon. Before you run out for plants and oils, however, you should smudge your home to clear out any negative energy.

Select your house plants with care. Round-leaf plants are friendlier symbolically than, say, cacti or any plants with pointed leaves.

Jade plants are excellent choices. They do well indoors, especially if near a window, have gently rounded leaves, and represent wealth, prosperity, and happiness.

Place your house plants with the same care with which you selected them. Usually, every room has several "power spots" where plants seem to flourish. Quite often, the family pet will snooze in or near power spots. Or you may sense them on your own. As you place your house plants, request that they bring happiness into your home.

Freshly cut flowers enhance the energy in any home. Select flowers that are brilliantly colored or that seize your attention.

✳ Wiccan Wonderings: How can you boost a home's positive energy?

We often know instinctively when our homes need an infusion of energy. It's mostly common sense. We paint things a different color, rearrange or buy new furniture, clear clutter, or repair what doesn't work. All of these things shift energy. You can also smudge the rooms, then burn a white scented candle in each room, allowing them to burn out naturally. Follow this with a brief meditation requesting that harmony and happiness enter the house. ✦

You don't have to have incense or oils burning constantly in your home to invite happiness inside. You might simply light one or the other as you're placing the plants in your house and arranging the fresh flowers.

Making these small gestures toward inviting happiness into your home—and thus, into your life—might inspire you to go even further. Do any of the rooms need to be painted? Are blinds broken or curtains torn? Maybe it's time for a general facelift.

The People and Pets at Home

The people and pets who share your living space contribute to the overall feeling texture of your home. If you have a roommate or someone else in your home with whom you don't get along or who is mostly negative, then you need to take measures to rid the rooms of that negativity. This may call for a sage smudging at regular intervals: Do so once a week for a month, then once a month after that. Other remedial adjustments might also be in order. You can include a piece of onyx or burn a black candle in or near the person's room to absorb the negative energy. If you burn a black candle, let it burn all the way down, then toss it out. You don't have to throw out the onyx; just bathe it in sea water (or water with some sea salt in it if you don't live near an ocean) and then set it in the sun for a few minutes to charge it.

If you have a pet who is hostile toward you or other people, you might try a little feng shui magick. Locate the family area of your home. This area lies in the eastern part of the house or, in Western feng shui, the farthest left-hand side of your house when you stand inside your front door. Add a tabletop fountain to the family area, a couple of jade plants, and something black. And, of course, don't forget to give your pet plenty of love.

If you have children, the best area in feng shui lies in the Western part of the house or, if you're standing in the front door, directly opposite the family area. If your kids are hostile or angry, use anything yellow in that area—flowers (with round leaves), curtains, linen, quilts, whatever feels right. Symbols for children and creativity are also good here, as are music, bells, and lights.

Once the negativity in the children's area is purged, put a white crystal or white flowers somewhere in the room. It helps to balance emotions.

Selling Your Home Quickly

Few things are more frustrating than putting your house on the market and then having it sit there, month after excruciating month, with no progress. There are always dozens of rational excuses for why a house hasn't sold—the wrong time of year, rising interest rates, the house needs work, the neighborhood isn't close enough to schools. But it only takes one person to buy your home, and a little help from the universe doesn't hurt!

If you're trying to sell your home and could use a boost, begin with a smudging, using sage. Start in the room that is visible as you step in the front door, then smudge in each of the four directions, followed by the doorways, baseboard, windows, closets, and everything else. Repeat this process in every room, then proceed to the next spell.

✳ **Wiccan Wonderings: What should you do when your house won't sell?**

To sell your home, you must be ready to release it and let go emotionally. Until you can imagine yourself living elsewhere without regrets, no spell in the universe will help. Make peace with your home, expressing your gratitude toward it for having sheltered and protected you. This might feel odd, but do it anyway. Spend a few minutes in each room, remembering good experiences and smudging each room as you walk through. Then watch how things will unfold. ✦

A Spell to Sell

Tools:
1 gold candle
1 red candle
Your favorite oil
When: During a Waning Moon

Before you even list your house with a realtor or put out that "for sale" sign, light your oil burner with your favorite oil inside. Place a red candle on one side of the burner and a gold on the right. As you light each one, say:

My house sells quickly
For at least (state the price you want).
Make it so.

Repeat it throughout the Waning Moon period. Allow the candles to burn out naturally.

A Spell to Find a Home

Tools:
Paper, pen, glue, scissors, a poster board
When: The Full Moon

You can either sketch the house you're looking for or find pictures or photographs that depict the house and create a wish board. A wish board consists of a poster board covered with photos, pictures, sayings, and affirmations that relate to one or several different goals and desires. It's a powerful visualization device, especially when you put the poster somewhere so visible that you can't help but see it.

The idea is to create a visual tool for what you desire. Make it vivid and detailed. Get the rest of the family involved. Kids love doing this sort of thing and often come up with things you didn't think of. The more energy that is poured into the desire, the quicker it will materialize.

A Spell to Protect Your House

A word of caution about this spell. In one sense, it implies a belief in victimization. However, there are times when we feel better knowing that the odds are stacked in our favor, so if you use the spell in that spirit, it can be applied to any number of situations.

Tools:
Cedar oil
Animal totem
When: Whenever you feel the need

The totem you select should be that of an animal with which you feel a kinship and represents protective power to you. Light your burner and when the scent begins to billow from it, pass the totem through it and say:

Protect this home,
High to low,
Fence to fence,
Door to door,
Light to dense,
Roof to floor.

Moving into a New Home

Any kind of move entails a monumental shift in energy. You are shifting gears not only in the physical world, but on a metaphysical level as well. Quite often, moves coincide with other major life events and experiences—births, marriages, divorces, death, work transfers, or new jobs. Not only do you have to contend with the physical logistics, but there are psychological adjustments as well. Whether the move is a few miles away or across the country, it can be stressful for everyone involved. Even when a move goes smoothly, you're faced with the daunting task of unpacking your belongings at the other end. Spells can help ease the stress.

A Spell to Ensure a Smooth Move

Every Friday night for the month before you move, burn some basil oil or burn a sprig of chamomile. The first promotes harmony and the second blesses a person, place, or thing. As you light both, vividly imagine your move going smoothly and seamlessly, with everything clicking into place and unfolding according to plan.

If at all possible, it's wisest not to move when Mercury is retrograde. When a planet is going retrograde, it means that from our viewpoint here on earth, it appears to be moving backward through the Zodiac. Since Mercury rules communication and travel, glitches usually show up when the planet is retrograde. Check with an astrologer or on any of the astrology sites on the Web for the periods when Mercury is retrograde.

✦ Wiccan Wonderings: What's the best way to bring good luck to a new home?

The first things you should bring into your new home are a loaf of freshly baked bread, a bottle of wine, and a new broom. The bread and wine ensure that you will always have enough to eat and drink in your new home. The broom represents the hearth—and the sweeping away of negative energy that the former tenants may have left behind. ✦

Parting Thoughts about Home

Become more aware of how you enter and leave your home. Do you arrive or depart in anger, slamming doors and muttering to yourself? Or do you arrive and depart with respect for the space itself? Do you take off your shoes when you enter your house? In Japan, the removal of shoes is considered respectful.

Whether arriving or departing, you are imbuing the house with your energy. If the energy is angry, hostile or sad, then over a period of time that becomes the dominant energy in the house. If, on the other hand, the energy is upbeat and happy, *that* becomes the dominant energy. When you live with other people, of course, you can't control how they feel within the house. But at least you can make them more aware of how they enter and leave.

A home with kids, pets, and live plants is apt to be filled with lively, upbeat energy. The chi also flows better. Live plants are telling about the general mood in the house. If they flourish, then the dominant energy is probably upbeat and positive.

If you work at home, then it's even more important to keep the dominant mood in your house upbeat and positive. Develop awareness of and respect for the place where you live, and your life there will be much more enjoyable.

Chapter 15

Spells for Travel

IF YOU FLY COMMERCIALLY at all, you're no doubt familiar with this scenario. You arrive at the airport an hour or more ahead of your flight, check your bags, and half an hour later find out the flight is going to be delayed several hours—or worse, canceled.

Maybe you're fortunate and your flight leaves on time, but every seat is filled and you're crammed in a window seat, next to someone who sneezes constantly during the flight or has a crying baby. To make things worse, the guy in front of you lowers the back of his seat all the way down, so that your knees are nearly crammed under your chin.

Welcome to air travel in the twenty-first century. Even if you arrive at your destination on time, the physical discomforts of air travel are often considerable and they, in turn, create emotional turmoil. Is there any way to mitigate the effects?

Extending Your Energy Field for Travel

To counter space constraints on a flight, your best bet is to extend your aura. People generally sense each other's boundaries and if your energy extends several feet from your body, it's less likely that someone will violate your personal space.

Ten or fifteen minutes before you board your flight, sit with your feet flat on the floor and focus on the tips of your shoes. Stare until your vision begins to blur, then imagine yourself in a cocoon of white light.

The cocoon should encompass all of you, from the tips of your toes to the top of your head. At first the cocoon may be small, extending a few inches from your body. Imagine the cocoon expanding, filling with even more light. Color the light if you want—any color except black will work. Imagine the cocoon of light expanding until it stretches several feet from your body in all directions.

When you feel the energy has expanded to where you want it, silently repeat: *I am safe, protected, and comfortable throughout my flight.* Repeat this several times. Then give tell yourself that every time you repeat this phrase, your energy field will automatically expand so that it stretches at least two or three feet from your body.

During your flight, repeat the phrase whenever you feel the need. If you do this when you're jammed in a window or middle seat, the person next to you is going to feel it. The person may shift his body away from yours. If you maintain the cocoon at several feet, the person may even get up and move to another seat—if there are any.

Dealing with the Person in Front of You

The first thing to do when you feel cramped by the person in front of you is calm yourself. Resist the urge to jackknife your legs against the seat. Maintain your extended aura. Shut your eyes and focus on your heart. Visualize waves of soft, pale light pouring from your heart's energy center. Extend the waves until they spill over the seat in front of you. Imagine the waves of light surrounding the person in front of you. When you feel reasonably sure that the light surrounds the person, silently request that he put his seat up.

✴ **Wiccan Wonderings: What should you do to prepare for a road trip?**
Before you pull out of your driveway, take sixty seconds to surround your car with light. White light is probably the best because it's a symbol for protection, but pastels work, too. Avoid black and brilliant colors. Imagine the light as a rubbery cocoon. Trust that you will glide along inside your cocoon through traffic both thick and sparse. ✦

Repeat your request several times. If this doesn't work, extend the light even farther. Your success is dependent on how vividly you can imagine the light.

A word of caution about the light: sometimes it makes the other person fall asleep.

Calming a Crying Baby

Infants are sensitive to the change in atmospheric pressure on a plane, and it's likely that crying may help them clear their ears. If you're seated next to or near a crying infant, the surest way to ease the child's misery—and thus your own—is to work from the heart energy center.

Once again, imagine light pouring from your heart center. It can be any pastel color. Let the light surround the child, cradling it. When you feel the child within the light, rock the light gently, as though you were holding the child in your arms. Whisper to the child in your mind. Keep this up for several moments even after the child stops crying.

A Spell for Traveling During the Waxing Moon

Tools:
1 white candle
Rosemary, oil or herb
Rose quartz
When: As needed, within twenty-four hours before your departure

If you're going to be traveling when the moon is waxing, this spell should be done the day before you leave. It's more powerful if you do it at night, but it can be done during the day as well.

Light the rosemary. As you light the white candle, say:

In the light of the growing moon,
I am protected and blessed in my journey,
And arrive at my destination soon.

A Spell for Traveling During the Waning Moon

Tools:
1 white candle
1 gold candle
White flower in a bowl of water
When: As needed, or twenty-four hours before your departure

The Waning Moon is a time of decrease, so you need a bit of a boost when traveling under this moon phase. The white flower you use in this spell should be broken off just below the bud, so the petals float on the surface of the water. Any kind of white flower can be used.

As you light the candles, imagine that any negativity associated with your trip is absorbed by the flower. Then say aloud:

As time does tell,
My journey goes well.
So mote it be.

Creating Space in Your Head

This visualization technique works for claustrophobia, but also mitigates fear, near-panic, anxiety, and high emotions. Center yourself with a couple of deep breaths, then create a mental image of a wide-open space—the beach, the ocean, a field, a park, or even an open road. If you imagine somewhere that has personal significance to you, the visualization will be more vivid. When, for instance, you imagine your favorite beach, you can almost feel the hot sand against your bare feet, smell the scent of salt in the air, see the blue perfection of the water, and hear gulls screeching through the sunlight. The more personal the image, the better it works.

The tricky part is holding the image long enough to convince your body and emotions that the crisis has passed. But with practice, nearly anyone can do it.

Other Types of Travel

So far, we've concentrated on air travel. But, depending on where you're going and who you're with, travel by car can also be stressful. Any parent who travels by car with young children knows that it can be stressful. *Are we there yet? I have to go to the bathroom. I'm bored.* Writer Nancy Pickard, however, had a more specific challenge. When her son was very young, he used to get car-sick.

She was reading Louise Hay at the time, and Hay said that the probable emotional cause of motion sickness was a fear of being trapped, of not being in control. Instead of trying to reason with her son about why he shouldn't feel trapped or afraid in the car, she came up with another solution. Every time her son started to feel sick in the car, she would start singing, "I am in control." Her son would start singing it, too, and pretty soon the motion sickness passed.

A playful approach to fear or problems often dissolves the underlying emotion before it can take root and grow.

A skeptic might say that singing *I am in control* while a child is about to vomit in your back seat doesn't change anything. That same skeptic would probably also say that affirmations, visualizations, and spells are just spit in the wind. Doubt is easy—maybe one of the easiest things any of us do. It's much tougher to try something that contradicts your beliefs about what is possible just to see what happens.

Your Travel Charm

The charm you use when you travel should contain fewer items than charm bags you use at home. It's a good idea to carry it close to your body. There should be at least one item inside which, when you touch it, communicates a strong sense of safety and protection. ✦

Quite often, the best time to take the leap is when you travel by car: a long road trip or a trip to the grocery store or to Little League—the where is less important than the trying. So start small. The next time you're circling a parking lot in search of a parking space, *create the space in your head*. See the parking space, see yourself pulling into it, trust that it'll happen.

This type of manifestation is probably one of the simplest to do, if your desire is strong enough. Try it yourself.

A Spell for Smooth Sailing

This spell is great for travel in general, but is especially good for long distance air travel, foreign or domestic.

> *Tools:*
> 1 white candle
> Your favorite herb or aromatic oil
> Object that represents your trip
> *When:* Twenty-four hours before your departure

The day before your departure, light your herb or burner. As the scent permeates the air, light the candle and say aloud:

> *By this flame's bright light*
> *My trip to (name destination)*
> *Unfolds smoothly, on time, without blight.*
> *Make it so.*

Pass the object through the smoke of the herb or oil, then snuff out the candle and toss it out.

Your Traveling Magick Kit

Kids operate under the wisdom of taking a blanket or toy with them when they travel. These objects help them acclimate to a new place because they're familiar and comforting. Your traveling magick kit is meant to fill the same function.

Here are some suggestions about what to include in your kit:

1. Your favorite stone
2. A couple of sticks of your favorite incense
3. A perfume whose scent puts you in a calm, meditative state
4. A small candle
5. A travel-size, unopened container of sea salt
6. A journal to record dreams, experiences, random thoughts

You can even include some other small, personal item that has special significance to you. Then, whenever you're stuck in traffic, or in some other stressful travel situation, simply touching the item will help to calm you down. Your magick tools might vary from trip to trip. But you should probably have at least one object that's a staple.

Chapter 16

Spells for Kids

MOST KIDS POSSESS an innate understanding of magick. They lose a tooth and the Tooth Fairy leaves them money under their pillows. On Christmas Eve, they put out cookies for Santa Claus and the cookies are gone in the morning. They toss a penny into a fountain and make a wish, certain the wish will come true. We are all born into magick. The difference between kids and adults is that kids haven't forgotten it.

Preteens and teens can do these spells alone, if they're so inclined, but they're more fun to do with friends. An adult can do the spells with younger kids—or with older kids, if they'll let you! These spells are simple and can be done at any time, on any day, under any phase of the moon. There aren't any rules. If you're doing the spells along with the kids, remember to mention intent and passion. Children have an abundance of both, and because they love make-believe, they tend to throw all their energy into spells. Don't be surprised if you, the adult, learn a thing or two by watching how they immerse themselves in the process.

✳ Wiccan Wonderings: Are spells safe to do with kids?

Kids generally enjoy casting spells, especially if it's done in a spirit of fun and adventure, and parents or other authority figures haven't attached any stigma to it. If you're a parent and are casting these spells with your kids, you'll find that it deepens your closeness. Perhaps that's the real magick. ✦

Balloon Magick

Tools:
1 balloon
Helium
Sheet of paper
Pen with the appropriate colored ink
Colored ribbon
When: When you feel like it

This spell is great for any occasion. Before you even get started, decide on what color ribbon you want to use to tie your balloon. Make it an adventure. Go to a fabric or drug store and let your child pick out the color of the ribbon and the ink of the pen you both will use to write down your wish.

Next, select a colored balloon for every person who's going to do the spell. Each of you should choose your own color, so you'll be able to differentiate the balloons once they're in the air.

You're going to need helium to fill the balloons. Check out stores that carry party supplies for kids. Once you've got the helium, you should all jot down your wishes on separate sheets of paper, in the color of ink you selected. Keep your wishes simple.

Roll up the sheets of paper, insert each one into the appropriate balloon, and fill the balloons with helium. Each person should tie off the balloon with the colored ribbon selected. Go outside to a place where you have a clear view for at least several miles—a beach, a hill, a field, a park. Here, say your wish out loud and release the balloon.

The higher the balloon goes before you lose sight of it, the greater the chances of your wish coming true.

Magickal Objects

When Swiss psychologist Carl Jung was a child, he found a smooth stone, which he kept in a matchbox. He confided in the stone. He told the stone his deepest secrets. He carried it around with him. Years later, in his autobiography, *Memories, Dreams, Reflections,* Jung movingly described his experiences with this stone, the magick that he associated with it, the power with which he imbued it.

And that's the key with any power object: It is powerful only because we make it so. Its magick originates in us, with our intent and our passion. But first, you have to find your power object.

What type of object appeals to you? That's the first thing to decide. Rocks, driftwood, an animal figure made of fabric, ceramic, stone, wood, even plastic: Any of these are fine. The object should be three-dimensional—as opposed to a picture of a stone or a piece of driftwood—and should have some sort of personal meaning. It should also be small enough to carry with you—in a pocket, a purse, a backpack.

Crystals and certain gemstones make excellent power objects. So do figures of angels, unicorns, and mythical Gods and Goddesses. Just about anything three-dimensional and small enough to carry can serve as a magickal object *if* it feels right.

Imbuing the Object with Power

Once you've found your object, you have to imbue it with power. There are several ways to do this. You can sleep with the object under your pillow for a night, hold it tightly in your hands and let your energy suffuse it, or carry it around with you for several days. If you select a crystal, wash it in sea water first, then hold it up to the sunlight and state what you would like the crystal to do.

With children, who are eager to get on with it, it's best to have them hold the object in their hands for a few moments and state out loud what they would like their power object to do. Once the object is imbued with power, you're ready to try it out with a spell.

Bubble Magick

Tools:
Bottles of bubbles
Your power object
Your imagination
When: Any time, but a Full Moon is best

Part of the secret of manifesting anything is to engage your imagination as well as your emotions. Kids know this instinctively, but somewhere along the way to adulthood, we forget it. Spells like this one and the balloon magick spell help us remember.

On a breezy night on the Full Moon, take your power object and bottles of bubbles to a hill, field, or park—someplace wide open. Place your power object on the ground in front of you, then make a wish and blow your bubbles. Your wishes are now inside the bubbles. Your power object and the breeze are going to carry the bubbles high into the air, where the Gods and Goddesses will hear the wishes—and grant them.

As the bubbles with your wishes inside rise into the moonlit sky, say the following:

My wishes travel
Through the light to you
Whole and protected
The entire night through.

A Wish Spell

Tools:
Your power object
Sheet of paper and a pen
1 gold candle
When: Any time

Write your wish on a sheet of paper, sign and date it, and place it under your power object. Keep your wish simple and straightforward. As you light the gold candle, say:

My wish goes out
Free of doubts,
Its travel lit by the flame
That bears my name.

Let the candle burn down naturally, then toss it out, thus releasing your wish.

Making a Magick Box

Most stage magicians have a box, the kind from which a dove emerges, or in which the woman lies as the magician saws her in half. The Magick Box we're talking about here, though, is for *real* magick.

Spells, Kids, and Creativity

Casting a spell is an endeavor that's just as creative as sketching a picture or writing a story. As an experiment, ask your child to think of something she really wants. Then work with her to create an appropriate spell. Concoct potions that you can actually drink. Break out the crayons, paint, and construction paper. And, as the adage goes, release your own inner child in the process. ✦

Everyone in the family can participate in this one. You'll need a shoebox or a similar container that's small enough to fit on a shelf, but large enough to accommodate the things you're going to put into it. Make it colorful by painting it, coloring on it, pasting shapes or pictures on it. The point is to personalize it.

The words *The Magick Box* should be written on the box in a prominent place. Put the box in an area where everyone in the family has access to it and can see it when they enter the house. When the box is completely decorated and in place, everyone in the family should write down one wish, sign and date it, and read it aloud to the others. Then it goes into the box.

Sharing your wishes with each other galvanizes the family's collective energy. This builds momentum and attracts what you want more quickly. Once a week or so, go through the wishes in the Magick Box and read them aloud again. As the wishes come true, remove them from the box. Someone in the family should keep a master record of each wish, the date it was put into the box, and the date it came true. This gives you a clear idea of how long it takes to manifest what you want.

Sometimes, we have wishes that we may not want to share with other people. These can go into a personal magick box in your room. It's important to date these wishes, too, so that you have some idea of how long it takes to get your wish.

As with any spell or visualization, if nothing happens within a reasonable amount of time, you should simplify your wish or reword it. It's important for kids to understand that their wishes should be realistic. If your son is wishing for an A in science but his grades are Ds across the board, then a more realistic wish would be that he gets the help he needs in science to bring up his grade. He also has to be willing to do the work required to raise his grade. If he wishes for an A but isn't willing to make the effort, then he's missing the point about the Magick Box. It's fine to make wishes, but you have to be willing to back up your wish with effort in the real world.

Wishing for a Pet

Even if your family has enough pets or no pets or people in the household are allergic to pets, one child's wish can bring a pet into your home. Children don't need to do a spell or an affirmation or any of the things you're supposed to do to get your wish. Without realizing it, when wishing for a pet, they do the most important things. They back their wish with such passion and need, and often create a vivid visual depiction in their mind to reflect their wish. In this way, they often draw a pet to them, so never underestimate the power of a child's wish! ✦

Dream Magick

Before your child goes to sleep at night, have her say her wish aloud three times. She should request a dream that expresses her wish, and the request should be said once aloud and again to herself. She should also make a suggestion to herself that she remember the dream when she has it.

She may have to repeat this several nights in a row, but she'll eventually have a dream that expresses her wish. When she relates it to you, question her about the details. Was the dream in color? Who was in it? What was going on? What time of the year was it? These details often hold clues about when the wish will come true and in what form it will appear.

A Spell for School

Nothing can make a child's life more miserable than a teacher with control issues or one who should be in some other profession because he or she really doesn't enjoy kids. Teachers like this can make children feel powerless and humiliated, and turn them off to school.

The next bit of magick is to remedy a situation with a troublesome teacher—without causing any harm to the teacher.

Write down the specific problem you're having with a teacher. "I'm not doing well in Mr. Horn's class." Or: "Ms. Jennings picks on me." On a separate sheet of paper, write the opposite. "I'm doing great in Mr. Horn's class." Or: "I communicate well with Ms. Jennings."

Take the piece of paper on which you wrote the problem and bury it in your yard. Tape the other sheet of paper—what you want to have happen—on your mirror or someplace else where you'll see it often.

Trust that the situation will be resolved in a short period of time.

A Friend Spell

This spell is great for making new friends. Blow up a dozen balloons of different colors. Use a bike pump, if you have one. Tie different colored ribbons around each balloon, decorate them with magic markers, and on each one write "new friend."

Tie the balloons to trees in your yard, put them in your room, on your porch, wherever they're visible to you. Before the balloons are deflated completely, you'll have new friends.

A Spell for Bringing Lost Pets Home

Like adults, kids experience many kinds of love, and one of the strongest and most enduring involves the animals in their lives. Pets that are happy and loved don't have any reason to leave home. But animals sometimes get disoriented, especially after a move. Since this spell involves the use of candles, children should have an adult present.

> *Tools:*
> Photo of your pet or an effigy that symbolizes it
> Pinch of vervain
> Pinch of myrrh
> Pinch of sage
> 4 white candles
> *When:* As needed

Put the photo of your pet or its effigy in a prominent place. Place four white candles around it. Sprinkle the herbs around the picture or effigy. As you light the candles and the incense, hold a mental image of your pet. Visualize your pet coming home safely, in good health. Feel the joy you'll experience when this happens. Get your feelings behind it, then say the following:

> *(Name) comes home to me,*
> *so mote it be.*
> *(Name) comes home to me*
> *healthy, protected, and safe,*
> *no longer a little waif.*

(Name) comes home to me,
through the power of three,
so mote it be.

Let the candles burn out on their own. Keep your pet's photo or effigy displayed until your animal returns home. Then bury it in the backyard, so that your animal will always remain close to home.

Charms for Kids

Children of all ages generally enjoy making charms. Their concerns usually revolve around school and their friends and social lives—their business world—so the same guidelines can be followed. However, a child's charm bag should contain fewer objects and serve a specific purpose.

✳ Wiccan Wonderings: What types of tarot decks can kids use?

Many children have an instinctive grasp of what tarot cards mean; the artwork speaks to them. There are more than 300 tarot decks on the market, and some are suitable for children of all ages. The miniature Ryder-Waite deck costs about $10, and kids like the size. *The Unicorn Tarot* appeals to a child's sense of magic. *The Aquarian Tarot* appeals to teens. *The Inspiration Tarot*, a blank deck that allows you to design your own cards, is perfect for kids who are aspiring artists.

Suppose, for instance, that your child is having problems with math and with her math teacher. She must first ask herself what she wants to accomplish. Does she want a better relationship with the teacher? Does she want the teacher to be more helpful? Less intimidating? She has to identify the problem, then pinpoint her desire concerning the teacher and the subject.

Once she has done that, she should decide on the color of the bag. Encourage your child to use her intuition in selecting a color and cotton or silk fabric. If she doesn't want to make her own bag, check out stores that stock them. She should keep the number of objects she chooses for her bag to three or four. Limiting the number means that she has to give more thought to each object she selects.

For a charm that addresses issues with a particular subject, at least one item should be something related to the subject. For math, it could be an equation jotted on a sheet of paper or a string of numbers or even a geometric shape. For teacher issues, include one item that is related to the teacher—his or her name on a piece of paper, the room number for the class, even a sketch of the teacher. The other objects would relate your child's desire about resolving the issue.

The creation of the charm bag should always be done in a spirit of fun because the spirit with which the bag is made becomes part of its magic. Also, remind your child—and yourself—that magick doesn't happen unless you also take action toward the end that you desire. In terms of the math example, a spell won't solve your child's difficulties with math unless your child also studies the subject.

Creating Your Own Spells

Kids usually enjoy creating their own spells. There are, however, some simple guidelines to follow, which you should impress upon your kids before creating spells.

1. **Harm no one.** Remember, this is the prime directive of spell-casting. It extends to all life and applies to the earth as well.
2. **Believe that what you're doing is possible.** Without this belief, no spell will get results.
3. **Be clear about your intent and goal.** Always ask yourself: Exactly what do I want?
4. **Back your spell with positive emotion.** Emotion shifts energy. The more heightened the emotion, the more positive it is, the quicker you'll get results.
5. **Keep your request simple.** "I want an A in math, a date to the prom with Jim, and a car for my birthday." That's the opposite of simple. Stick to one request.

6. **If you're doing a spell for another person, make sure you have that person's permission.** This is an important facet of any spell you cast. Even if you're trying to help someone else, even if you have the person's best interests at heart, *always ask.*

7. **Have fun.** Spells should always be done in the spirit of fun and adventure. They're meant to be empowering, and part of empowerment is enjoying what you're doing while you're doing it.

8. **Before doing a spell, open with a prayer of protection for yourself and others.** You can draw your prayer from a traditional religion, or it can be a personal one that you create with your kids. Make this prayer your opening ritual.

9. **Don't give up.** If your spells don't seem to be working, follow the remedies suggested earlier. Revise your spells, reword them, develop an inner awareness of what you're doing and why.

10. **Read, read, read.** Nonfiction books about magick and spellcasting will bolster your practical skills. But fiction will make you feel the magic. Encourage your kids to read the *Harry Potter* books; J.R.R. Tolkien's *Lord of the Rings* trilogy; Marion Zimmer Bradley's *Avalon*, about Camelot; *The Forever King*, by Warren Murphy and Molly Cochran; or *The Chronicles of Narnia*, by C. S. Lewis.

Parting Thoughts on Witchcraft and Spells

NOW THAT YOU'VE LEARNED about casting a Circle, choosing ingredients, and creating spells, you have many tools to assist you on your journey toward incorporating magick into your life. Before you finish this book, take a moment to reflect on some spellcraft basics, and be sure to keep them in mind in all of your work. Remember, all of those guidelines you just reviewed in Chapter 16 don't apply only to kids!

Ultimately, being a Witch is really about fulfillment. You will reach down into a part of yourself that has been neatly tucked away, awaken the magick there, and then bring it back into your daily life. You will reclaim your birthright as a spiritual being, and accept your potential in the new role. Mind you, this won't always be easy. Other people won't always understand. Although it might create some difficulties in your life, exploring Wicca and practicing spellcraft will also change your life in incredible ways.

The ultimate goal of becoming a Witch or Wiccan is simply to live and be the magick. It won't happen overnight. It takes time, patience, willpower, and determination to reach that goal, but it is attainable. Along the way, the path might become bumpy, and some days you might feel as if nothing is happening at all. Don't get discouraged. In those quiet moments, you'll truly begin to reflect on and internalize what you're learning, and you'll take it to heart.

Be persistent, stay alert, and keep moving forward. Allow yourself to become what you already are in your heart and soul—a powerful, magickal, and spiritual person. Express that reality joyfully—live the magick, and be blessed.

Index